The Little Book
on
Legal Writing

Second Edition

Alan L. Dworsky

Fred B. Rothman & Co.
Littleton, Colorado 80127
1992

Library of Congress Cataloging-in-Publication Data

Dworsky, Alan L.
  The little book on legal writing / Alan L. Dworsky — 2nd ed.

    p.   cm.
  Includes bibliographic references (p.   ).
  ISBN 0-8377-0560-6
  1. Legal composition.   2. Law—United States—Language.
I. Title.
KF250.D88   1992
808'.06634—dc20   92-8448
                                                      CIP

Second Printing 1994

Printed in the United States of America

In memory of my dad

Thanks to all who read and commented on the manuscript of this book: Anne McKinsey, Hennepin County District Judge; Professor Carol Swanson and Jim Coben, Clinical Instructor, Hamline University School of Law; my cousin Dan Simon, graduating this year from the University of Minnesota Law School; Sheila Jarrett and Shannon Wingrove, my editors at Rothman. Special thanks to my wife Betsy Sansby, whose painstaking and perceptive critique was a gift of love.

Contents

Contents

Detailed Table of Contents

1 Introduction

If you want to learn legal writing fast with a minimum of effort, this book is for you. You can read the whole thing in a few hours. Or you can nibble your way through a little at a time, because I've broken down each subject into bite-sized sections.

This book grew out of my experience teaching legal writing to first-year law students. Each piece of advice relates to a question lots of my students asked or a mistake lots of them made in their memos and briefs. The advice applies equally to other kinds of legal documents as well, such as contracts and pleadings. In fact, much of it applies to nonfiction writing in general, because good legal writing is simply good writing. And unless you have that rare case that could be won by a dog with a note in its mouth, good writing makes a difference.

I had fun writing this book. I hope you have fun reading it.

2 Plain English

Learning legal writing isn't like learning a foreign language.
It's true you'll have to learn a couple hundred or so legal terms
in your law courses. But except for those, the good news is:
You can become a good legal writer *using only the words you
already know.* You just have to learn to select and arrange them
differently.

Most of you naturally select and arrange your words fairly
well when you talk. But some strange force possesses you when
you sit down to write, inhibiting your better instincts. I know
about this from conferences with my students about their work.
Often I point to a particularly vague or confusing sentence and
ask "What were you trying to say?" Usually the answer I get is
clearer than what was written, so my next question is "Why
didn't you write that instead?" As you write, constantly ask
yourself what you are trying to say. Imagine yourself explaining
it to a friend who knows nothing about law. Then put that
down on paper. Next edit it to make it as concise as possible,
adding back legal terms where necessary.

This simple and direct style is almost the equivalent—with
a few modifications and careful editing—of talking on paper.
It's called "plain English," and it's the style now uniformly
taught in legal writing texts and courses. This chapter briefly
summarizes its basic principles.

Avoid legalese. Reading old cases in casebooks may give you
the impression that writing like a lawyer means sprinkling your
prose with *aforesaid* and *herein* and other such words. These
words are not genuine terms of art because they have no special
or precise legal meaning. They are now considered stilted and

2

archaic by almost every authority on legal writing and are derisively labeled "legalese." Don't imitate casebook legalese when you write a memo or brief. Live lawyers don't write like dead judges.

Use familiar, plain words. The most important thing you must understand about the readers of your legal writing—whether they be legal writing teachers, law professors, lawyers, or judges—is that they are busy. They won't run to the dictionary to look up an unfamiliar word. They'll skip over it, and your effectiveness will suffer. So don't inflate your prose beyond recognition with your thesaurus. If you must use an unfamiliar word because it's the perfect word for your purposes, define it on the spot.

Even if you've got a fancy word that your readers will understand, a plain word is usually clearer and stronger. Say *tell* instead of *apprise; go* instead of *proceed; start* or *begin* instead of *commence* or *initiate; show* instead of *evince; try* instead of *endeavor; happen* instead of *transpire.* Say *later* instead of *subsequently.* Say someone *answered yes* instead of *answered in the affirmative.* Test your writing by reading it out loud. If a word feels like metal in your mouth because you'd never use it in conversation, scrap it.

Omit needless words. This is the classic maxim from Strunk and White's *Elements of Style.* Make it your mantra. As an undergraduate writer, you may have impressed your teachers with sheer bulk. This doesn't work in law school or practice. Busy readers appreciate a concise memo or brief; it shows you have respect for their precious time. Strive for brevity without sacrificing completeness. Get to the point.

After you've cut the needless sentences from your memo or brief with a chainsaw, take a scalpel and go after the needless words within the remaining sentences. Every word should serve a purpose. Here are some specific ways to omit needless words

within sentences.   I have noted the pages where some are
covered in more detail:

Avoid wordy prepositional phrases:

    for the purpose of = to
    in close proximity to = near, close to
    in order to = to
    in order for = for
    in regard to = about, concerning, regarding
    in terms of = at, in, for, by, with, etc. (p. 34)
    in the event that = if
    in the vicinity of = near
    in view of the fact that = because (p. 39)
    on the part of = by
    with reference to = about
    with respect to = about, concerning, regarding (p. 41)

Avoid redundant phrases:

    the area of tort law = tort law
    ask the question = ask
    emergency situation = emergency
    free gift = gift
    general consensus = consensus
    null and void = void
    personal friend = friend
    true facts = facts (p. 40)
    unexpected surprise = surprise

Avoid needlessly abstract constructions using *nature, one,
process, level,* etc.:

    The allegations were serious in nature =
    The allegations were serious

    The allegations were serious ones =
    The allegations were serious

Litigation is an expensive process =
Litigation is expensive

At the trial court level =
In the trial court

Omit needless introductory words:

The law is that for a statement to be privileged
    it must be true =
For a statement to be privileged it must be true

It can be seen that Hill involved the same issue =
Hill involved the same issue

It would seem that proving fraud will be difficult =
Proving fraud will be difficult

She *is a woman who* has a good driving record =
She has a good driving record

It is probable that the judgment will be reversed =
The judgment will probably be reversed

It is important to note that = [just note it]

This memorandum addresses the issue whether =
    [just address it]

Avoid needless modifiers like *very, pretty, somewhat, rather:*

very important = important, critical, crucial
very big = big, huge, giant, enormous
pretty incredible = incredible
rather unusual = unusual
somewhat profound = profound

Avoid freezing the action in a noun (p. 8):

conduct an examination = examine
engage in the pursuit of = pursue

have a dialogue = talk
make a decision = decide
possess knowledge = know

Prefer active voice (p. 7):

An order was issued by the court =
The court issued an order

I've given many other suggestions throughout this book on ways
to omit needless words in specific situations. These specific
suggestions should help you get the general idea. Once you get
it, make the "Delete" key your friend.

Prefer short sentences and paragraphs. Short sentences are
easy to read. They're easy to write too. And if you're no expert
at syntax, they're safe. It's hard to go wrong in a short sentence.
But notice the rule says *"Prefer* short sentences," not "Use
only short sentences." Long sentences can be easy to read if
they're carefully constructed and logically divided. They also
break up the mechanical effect of too many short sentences in
a row. Good musicians vary the length of their phrases when
they improvise. Do the same with your sentences. Your writing
should be pleasing to the ear as well as the eye.
    You should also prefer short paragraphs. A paragraph break
is a resting place for the reader in the steep climb through your
memo or brief. Don't make the reader wait too long between
rests. If a paragraph is longer than half a page, look for a
logical place to divide it. Logical dividing places occur in
predictable places:
  • between the statement of a rule and the explanation of
    a case from which it comes;
  • between the explanation of a rule and its application to
    your facts;
  • between the application of each of several elements or
    factors from a rule;
  • between an argument and a counterargument.

Strive for balance in paragraph length. If you make your paragraphs too short, your writing can seem fragmented. One- and two-sentence paragraphs can add punch if used sparingly; if overused, they make the reader do too much work organizing your thoughts. Write paragraphs that are long enough to show the connections between related sentences, but not so long that they exhaust the reader.

Build your sentences around active verbs. A sentence in the active voice is often clearer, stronger, and more concise than the same sentence in the passive voice. You can use the passive voice, but only if you've made a conscious decision that it better suits your purposes in a particular situation. To make that conscious decision, you must recognize the difference between active and passive voice.

Here's an example of active voice:

Example 1
The police *searched* the house.

The action in the sentence moves forward from the subject ("the police") through the verb ("searched") to the object ("the house").

A verb in the passive voice is accompanied by some form of the verb *to be (is, are, was, were, has been,* etc.):

Example 2
The house *was searched* by the police.

So far no meaning has been lost, but the sentence is two words longer in the passive voice. All other things being equal, you should prefer Example 1 over Example 2 under the principle "omit needless words."

The real danger comes when the object is dropped from a sentence in the passive voice:

Example 3
The house was searched.

Example 3 omits information contained in Example 2—who searched the house. People often write like this when they're trying to avoid responsibility for their actions: "Mistakes were made." Don't drain the life from your sentences by writing like this unintentionally.

With practice you will learn to recognize when you're writing in the passive voice. Until then, after you've written something, go back and look for any form of the verb *to be*. If you find a passive construction, ask yourself whether it would be better in the active voice. Nine times out of ten, it will.

But even when the verb in a sentence is in the active voice, the sentence can still be wordy and indirect if the real action is frozen in a noun. In the following example, the action is frozen in the noun "request":

Example 4
The defendant made a *request* for a continuance.

Moving the action to the verb "requested" makes the sentence shorter and stronger:

Example 5
The defendant *requested* a continuance.

Sometimes you can't use plain English. Plain English isn't always appropriate. You may choose to be indirect to minimize unfavorable facts or law. If your client struck the victim four times, the passive voice de-emphasizes that fact:

Example 6
The victim *was struck* four times.

Of course, you have to admit it was your client who did the striking, but the passive voice softens the blows.

You may want to try to intimidate non-lawyers by writing the way they expect lawyers to write:

Example 7

Ms. Anderson has requested that I inform you that if you do not vacate the premises forthwith, she will be forced to institute legal proceedings against you.

Your boss may not allow you to use plain English in some situations. When I started filling out time sheets at my first law job, I made the mistake of writing entries such as "Talked to client by phone about case." My boss instructed me that in the future this was to be "Telephone conference with client re: litigation strategy." After that, I never talked to other lawyers in the firm about cases either. I had "intraoffice conferences."

3 Style

Legal memoranda and briefs require a style that's slightly more formal than pure plain English. So this chapter starts by explaining the few adjustments you'll need to make. Then it moves on to general matters of style that are particularly important in legal writing.

Do not use contractions. I get to use contractions in this book because it's my book and I can do whatever I want. Contractions give writing a natural and friendly tone. But they have traditionally been considered inappropriate in formal legal writing, so you can't use them except in quotations. Sorry.

Don't write in the first person. In an office memorandum, you sound most authoritative when you keep the focus off yourself and on the analysis. In a brief to a court, you're most persuasive when you sound objective, and you sound most objective when the judges forget you're there. So avoid *I*, *me*, and *my*.

Also avoid *we*, *us*, and *our* when writing to a court. They're usually acceptable in an office memo: "*we* can argue." But make sure you're talking about the real *we* of your law firm or your side. Don't use *we* when it's really just you, as in "*We* will now discuss" or "*We* will now examine." You're too old to have imaginary friends.

There are a couple ways to avoid the first person. They can be illustrated through variations on the following sentence from an office memo:

Example 8
I think Weithoff has the stronger argument on this point.

One way to avoid the personal pronoun here is to take it out of the sentence:

Example 9
Weithoff has the stronger argument on this point.

But if you put the "I think" in Example 8 because you weren't really sure and wanted to make it clear this was just your opinion, then you'll probably feel a little uncomfortable with Example 9. In that situation, rewrite the sentence to show your degree of certainty:

Example 10
Weithoff *probably* has the stronger argument on this point.

Whatever you do, don't replace first-person pronouns with stilted alternatives like *this writer*.

Avoid rhetorical questions. A rhetorical question is a question with an implied answer:

Example 11
Is it reasonable to expect a buyer to read a contract at a check-out counter?

Avoid questions like this. They can sound confrontational or sarcastic. And if you leave it to the reader to supply an answer, you may not get the one you want. Don't imply your point; spell it out.

Don't use slang unless you're quoting. Slang is inconsistent with the formal tone of a memo or brief. Don't say the plaintiff's car was "totaled"; say "wrecked." Don't say the defendant "ripped off" the stereo; say "stole." Don't say the defendant was "smashed"; say "drunk" or— if it's the standard under a statute—"intoxicated."

You can use slang when you're quoting, even if it's offensive or obscene. In fact, if the other side said something in slang that helps your case, you may want to quote it over and over. For example, assume you represent the plaintiff in a fraud case.

If the defendant testified that the transaction was only some "honest scamming," you might look for opportunities to refer to the defendant's "scamming." Whenever you can, use the other side's words to make your case.

Get serious. Litigation is no laughing matter. A joke—even a funny one—may make the judges think you aren't serious about your case. If you treat your case lightly, chances are so will they. That's too big a risk to take for a laugh.

You may think you can put a joke in an office memo because you know your boss likes your sense of humor. But you should test every word you write with the question: "Would I be comfortable if my client—or a judge—read this?" More and more clients are switching lawyers midstream and taking their files with them or—worse yet—suing their lawyers for malpractice. Suddenly your clever memo is "Exhibit A." And suddenly you wish you hadn't referred to your firm's client as "the whiner."

Avoid footnotes. Footnotes sidetrack the reader. Taking a detour to the bottom of a page and back up again wastes time and breaks a reader's concentration. You're not writing a treatise or law review article, where footnotes may support a scholarly theory or guide the reader to sources for further research. You're trying to help your boss or a judge make a specific decision. If something is important enough to be included in your memo or brief, put it in the text.

Underline for emphasis sparingly. Don't print words you want to emphasize in bold, italics, or all capital letters. Underline them. As the written equivalent of raising your voice, underlining can make your writing more dynamic when used sparingly. But if you do it too much, it can irritate the reader, who may feel condescended to, shouted at, or badgered. And if you raise your voice about everything, you emphasize nothing. Like the boy who cried wolf, you eventually will be ignored.

Underlining for emphasis is most justifiable to emphasize critical language in a quotation. Show you've added emphasis by including the phrase "emphasis added" at the end of the citation. If the emphasis in your quotation was in the original—shown either by italics or underlining in the original—show that by including the phrase "emphasis in original" at the end of the citation.

If underlining is the equivalent of raising your voice, an exclamation point is the equivalent of shouting. Exclamation points are almost never used in legal writing.

Use conventional typeface. Many of you now have sophisticated word processors or printers that can produce a variety of typefaces. Lawyers have them too, but perhaps because the law is steeped in tradition, they have been reluctant to use new typefaces. Instead, most lawyers continue to use even the most expensive and sophisticated laser printers to produce memos and briefs that look as if they've been produced on a typewriter. That means generally the only typeface used is ordinary roman typeface. Underlining is used for emphasis and citations. Italics aren't used. Graphics aren't used either, such as little wedges or boxes before items enumerated on a list.

One typeface lawyers have started to use is boldface type. Bold works well for main headings (such as **ARGUMENT**) and point headings. But lawyers aren't yet using it for emphasis in the text of their memos or briefs. For that they're still underlining, so you should be too.

Use right justification only if your printer spaces evenly. When text is "right justified," all the lines are even on the right, like the lines in this book. Don't use right justification unless you've got a really good printer and word-processing program that spaces words evenly. Erratic or excessive spacing between words and sentences makes your writing harder to read. It also distorts citations, where precise spacing is important. If you've got an unsophisticated printer or word-processing program, turn right justification off.

Don't cheat on type size, line spacing, or margins. The people who will read your memos and briefs probably spend most of their time reading. Lawyers, judges, judicial clerks, and legal writing teachers all have tired eyes. When they read a memo or brief, they want to see nice big words on the page with plenty of space between the lines and at the margins.

Don't disappoint them. Check your typewriter, word processor, or printer to make sure your words are produced in ten- or eleven-point type (about the size of the words in this book). Also make sure your lines are fully double-spaced and your pages have one-inch margins on all sides. Your readers will know if you've cheated on any of these things to keep your memo or brief within a page limit, and they won't like it. Courts and teachers often have rules about these things, and can refuse to accept your memo or brief if it violates the rules. If you're over the page limit, omit needless words.

Avoid putting a heading at the bottom of a page. Traditionally, lawyers have not begun a new page for each section in a memo. Most begin a new page for each introductory section in a brief, such as the Questions Presented and Table of Authorities. Some begin a new page for the Statement of Facts and Argument in a brief. No one begins a new page for each point heading.

Whatever you do, avoid putting a heading at the bottom of a page. This is harder than it used to be. Computers allow you to type continuously without being conscious of page breaks and to insert material that alters where page breaks occur. And printers sometimes change the page breaks you saw on the screen. So you must go through your document immediately before—and after—you print it to make sure the headings are where you want them. If there aren't at least two lines of text under a heading, move it to the top of the next page. And if a heading isn't at the top of a page, make sure it stands out by putting an extra blank line or two before it.

Indent your paragraphs. Indent the first word of each paragraph five spaces. Then the reader can always tell whether the first line on a page begins a new paragraph.

Don't add extra blank lines between paragraphs. Paragraphs should be separated by a single blank line, which is the same amount of space there is between normal double-spaced lines.

Master the apostrophe. If you're like me, you squeaked through high school and college without ever learning to use the apostrophe properly. You may have been confused because usually the possessive of a word (*judge's*) and the plural (*judges*) sound the same. But even though they sound the same, you must indicate the possessive with an apostrophe.

The basic rules are simple. Form the possessive of a singular noun by adding an apostrophe followed by an "s" (*party's*); form the possessive of a plural noun by adding an apostrophe after the "s" (*parties'*):

Example 12
Each *party's* lawyer was present.

Example 13
All the *parties'* lawyers were present.

There are a couple exceptions to these rules. When a plural noun doesn't normally end in "s," add an apostrophe followed by an "s": *women's, men's*. If you wouldn't add another "s" or "z" sound to a singular noun, you can add just the apostrophe without an "s": *Court of Appeals'*. But if you would add another "s" or "z" sound, add an apostophe and an "s" to a singular noun even if it already ends in "s": *Congress's, witness's*.

Using the apostrophe when referring to more than one member of the same family often confuses students. If the family name is "Simpson" and you're talking about something that belongs to the family, the apostrophe goes *after* the added "s": "the *Simpsons'* house."

Attorney's fees and *attorneys' fees* are both acceptable. If you're trying to get fees under a statute, put the apostrophe wherever the statute puts it. Otherwise, use *attorney's fees* for one lawyer and *attorneys' fees* for more than one. Wherever you put the apostrophe, don't make attorney's fees your only goal in life. On their deathbeds, few lawyers say: "I wish I'd spent more time at the office."

Don't be a slasher. Don't make up ugly new words using the slash:

Example 14
Daly was a *professor/researcher* at Hamline University.

Try to make do with the few hundred thousand English words we already have:

Example 15
Daly was a *professor and researcher* at Hamline University.

Avoid "not un" combinations. Don't say "Congress was *not un*aware of the problem of sexual harassment when it enacted section 1983," say "Congress was *aware*." Don't say "*not un*familiar," say "familiar." Don't make the reader do the not unhard work of converting two negatives to a positive.

Don't write in headnote style. Don't drop the articles *a, an,* and *the.* This is done in headnotes—and telegrams, headlines, and want ads—to conserve space: "Buyer of Toyota sued dealer for negligence." But headnotes, besides being poor examples of English prose, aren't even good authority. You have enough room in a memo or brief to write real sentences. Put those articles back in: "*The* buyer of *a* Toyota sued *the* dealer for negligence." You don't want your writing to sound like a poorly dubbed Kung Fu movie.

Don't call someone a liar in a civil case. Lying is a sin. Criminal defendants have already been accused of sinning, so accusing them of lying is relatively insignificant. But in a civil case, saying someone *lied* is considered uncivil. Don't do it unless the evidence is indisputable. Say the other side *intentionally misrepresented* or *intentionally misstated*. These less emotionally charged substitutes soften the blow of the accusation and track the language of the relevant rules and statutes.

Talk about death without euphemisms. Homicide, wrongful death, wills and trusts— lawyers often deal with death. Euphemisms may be justified when you're talking with someone grieving the loss of a loved one. But in a memo or brief, talk about death directly. Say *death*, not *demise*. Say the person *died*, not *passed away* or *expired*. As nouns, *deceased* and *decedent* are acceptable because there is no plain English alternative. But you can often avoid these legalistic terms by instead using the dead person's name.

Talk about contracts correctly. Watch out for commonly misused words related to contracts. If an offer isn't accepted, it's *rejected* rather than *denied*. If it's accepted, the parties *enter into* a contract; they don't *enter* a contract. You could also say they *contracted with* each other. They are then *parties to a contract* or *contracting parties*. In the past, they might have been called *contractors*, but now that word is reserved for those in the construction business.

The nouns *contract* and *agreement* are synonyms. When parties agree to enter into a contract, they create an *express contract*, not an *expressed contract*. If the contract isn't written down, it's an *oral contract*, not a *verbal agreement*. "Verbal" simply means "in words," so technically it applies to both oral and written contracts.

Don't change what you call something. "Elegant variation" refers to the practice of changing what you call something so as not to bore the reader. It may have some literary merit, but in legal writing it's at best a distraction and at worst a source of confusion. Here's an example of what *not* to do:

> **Example 16**
> *The Toyota* entered the intersection after stopping at the stop sign. *The car* was accelerating when it was struck by the van. The impact caused *the vehicle* to roll over three times before coming to a stop upside down.

Although the writer was probably talking about the same car in all three sentences, it's impossible to tell for sure.

Be consistent. When you mention something more than once, call it the same thing or use a pronoun. Don't switch back and forth between a party's name and "Plaintiff" or "Defendant." If you announce there are three factors you are going to consider, and then start the first paragraph with "The first factor," don't switch at the start of the next paragraph to "The second consideration," and at the start of the next to "The third element." If you start with "factors," stick with "factors."

Some students think changing what they call people and things keeps their writing from becoming boring. But if their writing is boring, the problem lies elsewhere.

Maintain parallelism. In a sentence, words or phrases serving similar functions should match grammatically:

> **Example 17**
> Sally likes *swimming, walking,* and *running.*

This matching is called "parallelism." It's maintained in Example 17 because the three things Sally likes all end in "ing." "Sally likes swimming, walking, and *to run*" is bad grammar.

Parallelism isn't grammatically required between sentences that serve similar functions, but it makes your writing clearer and more cohesive. Suppose you want to show in four successive paragraphs that your case meets the four elements of fraud: material misrepresentation, intent, reasonable reliance, and damages. Identical phrasing in each topic sentence creates a pattern that's easy to spot and an argument that's easy to follow:

Example 18
The first element, material misrepresentation, is shown by . . . .
The second element, intent, is shown by . . . .
The third element, reasonable reliance, is shown by . . . .
The fourth element, damages, is shown by . . . .

Changing the phrasing breaks up the pattern and obscures the argument:

Example 19
Material misrepresentation, the first element, is shown by . . . .
The second element, intent, is established by . . . .
Reliance, which is the third element, is shown by . . . .
Fourth, the element of damages, is established by . . . .

You should also maintain parallelism in the sequence of sentences within parallel paragraphs. Suppose you want to give three pieces of information about three psychiatrists who examined your client. Give the information about each psychiatrist in the same order:

Example 20
Dr. Leah Rubinstien had been with the clinic for eight years. Dr. Rubinstien examined Smith three times. She diagnosed Smith as borderline psychotic.

Dr. Kenneth Chen had been with the clinic for six years. Dr. Chen examined Smith four times. He diagnosed Smith as manic depressive.

Dr. Andrea Wells had been with the clinic for twelve years. Dr. Wells examined Smith only once. She diagnosed Smith as schizophrenic.

In each paragraph, the first sentence tells how long the doctor has been with the clinic, the second tells the number of examinations, and the third tells the diagnosis. This makes the reader's job of comparing the psychiatrists easier.

Parallelism can make any relationship clearer. Maintain it be-

tween Questions Presented, point headings, case descriptions—
wherever a consistent pattern would help the reader. It can
even be used to add power and grace: "a government of the
people, by the people, and for the people." But mainly, parallelism binds your ideas together, so they won't be broken in
transit to the reader's mind.

Capitalize correctly. Don't capitalize every word having anything to do with law. The normal rules of capitalization apply
to legal writing. The few special rules can be found mainly in
practitioners' note P.6 in the *Bluebook*. I've summarized them
here.

> *Court.* *Court* should be capitalized when you're referring to
the United States Supreme Court or when you're giving the full
name of any other court:

Example 21
That issue was decided recently by the *Arizona Supreme Court.*

Court should also be capitalized when you're referring to the
court you're addressing:

Example 22
This *Court* should refuse to grant summary judgment.

Otherwise, *court* isn't capitalized:

Example 23
In Kelynack, the *court* held that sections 2-719(2) and 2-719(3)
are interdependent.

> *Litigation roles.* Litigation roles are capitalized when they
refer to the parties in your case:

Example 24
The *Defendant* in this case was properly served.

Litigation roles aren't capitalized when they refer to the parties
in a cited case:

Example 25
In <u>Kelynack</u>, the *defendant* was a motorcycle dealer.

Some lawyers use all capital letters for the names of their clients in documents submitted to a court:

Example 26
ALLIED STORES was not properly served.

This is unnecessary and unsightly. If God can get by with only one capital letter, so can your client.

Litigation documents. Capitalize the full titles of litigation documents in your case:

Example 27
Plaintiff has failed to respond to Sportco's *Request for Production of Documents.*

Don't capitalize informal references to litigation documents:

Example 28
Plaintiff has failed to respond to Sportco's *document requests.*

Governmental names. Once you've given the full name of a governmental department, officer, or act, you can usually shorten the name to a single word. Capitalize the shortened version:

Example 29
Appeals must be brought before the *Department of Human Services.* If the *Department* refuses to reinstate the benefits, the recipient can bring a civil action.

Similarly, the *Commissioner of Human Services* would become the *Commissioner*, and the *Animal Welfare Act* would become the *Act.*

Don't abbreviate the names of places. The abbreviations of geographical terms given in table T.10 in the *Bluebook* are used in citations, not in text. Write out the names of countries,

states, counties, and cities in full: "Los Angeles," not "L.A.";
"Flagstaff, Arizona," not "Flagstaff, AZ." Write out "United
States" in full unless you use it as an adjective: "U.S. economic
policy." Also write out the names of streets in full: "Torgerson
Street," not "Torgerson St."; "Walker Boulevard," not "Walker
Blvd."

But don't make the names of places fuller than they need to
be. "The state of California" has three needless words; it should
be simply "California." The only excuse for writing something
like "the state of X" or "the city of X" is to distinguish it from
something else with the same name: "Sportco is the largest
retailer of sporting goods in *the state of* New York."

Use proper style for numbers.   Rule 6.2 in the Bluebook
governs the use of numbers in legal writing. You should generally spell out the numbers zero through ninety-nine. If you want
to, you can also spell out round numbers like *hundred* and
million.   And you must spell out any number that begins a
sentence.   So if you have a number that's awkward to spell
out—like 1945—don't start a sentence with it.

Use numerals for dollar amounts and percentages if you're
using a lot of them. When you use numerals for dollar amounts,
use the dollar symbol ($) too; write "$4,500," not "4,500
dollars." Do the same with percentages; write "58%," not "58
percent." For an even dollar amount, there's no need to include a decimal point and two zeros; write "$10,000," not
"$10,000.00."

In citations, abbreviate the names of courts using ordinals,
as in "8th Cir." In text, spell out ordinals: "Eighth Circuit."

Lawyers often use both words and numerals for dollar
amounts in contracts to ensure no mistake is made:

Example 30
The buyer shall make four equal payments of *one hundred
thousand dollars ($100,000)* each.

Don't do this in a memo or brief.

Learn to tell time. For some unknown reason, time provides fertile soil for needless words. Use the single words on the right of this list instead of the wordy compound prepositions on the left:

> prior to = before
> subsequent to = after
> as of this date = today
> at a time when = when
> at the present time = now
> at this point in time = now
> at that point in time = then
> during the period when = when
> not later than = by
> until such time as = until
> up until = until
> two days before tomorrow = yesterday

Use the single words on the right of this next list instead of the redundancies on the left:

> advance planning = planning
> advance warning = warning
> continue on = continue
> early on = early
> later on = later
> now pending = pending
> past experience = experience
> predict in advance = predict

Dates. Dates are not abbreviated in a memo or brief. Write "November 13, 1992," not "Nov. 13, 1992" or "11/13/92." Some writing experts like the form "13 November 1992" because there's no comma and the numbers are separated, but it's not used in legal writing. That's fine with me, because I don't know how to say it, and I don't like the work of unscrambling it.

Don't add needless words to dates. "November 1992" is better than "November of 1992." "November 13, 1992" is better than "the 13th day of November, 1992." Don't use a phrase like "on or about" if you are reasonably certain of the date. Just say "on." Finally, don't use stilted phrases like "on the day in question." Say "on that day," "on the day of the robbery," "on Thursday," "on November 13," or whatever.

Avoid confusing the reader with too many dates. Give the full date of the first event in the facts you are recounting. Then drop the year from later dates if it's clear from the context that they occurred in the same year:

Example 31
Valdez left Los Angeles by car on April 12, 1992. On April 22, he reached Miami.

Another way to avoid giving the full date for the second event is to describe it in relation to the first:

Example 32
Valdez left Los Angeles by car on April 12, 1992. Ten days later he reached Miami.

Do this as much as possible when exact dates aren't important.

When you give a deadline, however, always give the exact date. For example, don't write in a letter: "You have ten days in which to accept this offer." Which ten days? Ten days from mailing? Ten days from receipt? Ten business days? If time is critical, avoid ambiguity by saying:

Example 33
If you want to accept this offer, I must receive a written acceptance from you at my office before 5 p.m. on August 17, 1992.

If the offeree is in a different time zone, add "Eastern Standard Time" or whatever.

Time of day. For giving the time of day, *a.m.* and *p.m.* are the abbreviations most commonly used, but *A.M.* and *P.M.* are also acceptable. Whichever pair you use, be consistent. You can use *o'clock* instead, but don't use it with *a.m.* or *p.m.,* as in "four *o'clock a.m.*" Phrases such as "four a.m. in the morning" are redundant. If it's clear from the context, simply say "at four."

Don't simultaneously specify a time and generalize it, as in "approximately 4:03 a.m." Round off the times you are estimating to the nearest hour, half hour, or at least quarter hour. And *about* means the same thing as *approximately* and has the virtue of being shorter.

Just as you should avoid confusing the reader with too many dates, avoid confusing the reader with too many times. Whenever possible, describe times in relation to one another. Say "ten minutes later," "earlier that evening," etc.

Gracefully avoid sexist language. Grammatically it is correct to use masculine singular pronouns—*he, him,* and *his*—to refer generically to persons of both sexes. But this is rightfully considered sexist language because it perpetuates the habit of thinking of the male as the model of a human being from which females deviate. And for a reader who thinks visually, the masculine pronoun will momentarily create the image of a man in the reader's mind. Test yourself on the following sentence:

Example 34
A lawyer should zealously represent his client.

Quickly now: What did the lawyer look like in your mind?

To counter the centuries-long oppression of women that sexist language has helped perpetuate, many academic legal writers have begun using only feminine singular pronouns to refer generically to persons of both sexes or have begun to alternate between the feminine and the masculine. This form of linguistic affirmative action is justifiable but distracting.

Even more distracting are ugly new constructions such as *he/she* and *s/he.* Don't use these. Also don't use *their* in place of a singular pronoun, as in the following incorrect sentence:

Example 35
A *lawyer* should zealously represent *their* client.

Their is plural and requires a plural antecedent. *Their* is wrong in Example 35 because its antecedent ("a lawyer") is singular.

Several techniques can help you avoid offending the reader with sexist language and distracting the reader with non-traditional language. A few of the most useful follow.

Take out the pronoun:

Example 36
A *lawyer* should zealously represent *the* client.

Switch to plural:

Example 37
Lawyers should zealously represent *their clients.*

Switch to second person:

Example 38
As a lawyer, *you* should zealously represent *your* client.

Use *his or her:*

Example 39
A *lawyer* should zealously represent *his or her* client.

Other techniques will work in some situations, such as substituting a gender-neutral pronoun (*one's*), repeating the noun, switching to passive voice, or rewriting the sentence entirely. No single technique will work in all situations. When you get stuck on a sentence, go through the possibilities. Generally choose the most economical solution. Use techniques that add words (like the clumsy *his or her*) as a last resort.

Old legal rules that talk about "the reasonable man" present a problem. Paraphrase them whenever possible so you can refer to "the reasonable person." If you must quote, you can substitute "person" in brackets for "man." Or you can leave the original as is and make the substitution in all your later references to the rule. The contrast makes the point without disrupting the flow of your memo or brief. On the other hand, putting "[sic]" after "man" in a quotation is heavy-handed and disruptive. Apply the principles in this paragraph by extension to old rules and statutes that use masculine pronouns.

Most other problems involving sexist language are easy to solve. Use gender-neutral terms for job titles: "police officer" instead of "policeman" or "policewoman," etc. Use *humankind, the human race,* or *human beings* instead of *man* or *mankind.* Avoid having to decide whether to use *Mrs., Ms.,* or *Miss* by eliminating these titles—and *Mr.*—from your writing. If you must use these titles, use them for everybody you talk about. Using them just for women— like opening doors only for women—is a vestige of inequality.

Finally, don't talk about a statute or rule being *emasculated.* If you must use a metaphor for physical disfigurement, say it was *eviscerated.*

4 Usage

This chapter contains words that are often misused in legal writing.

accrue, incur *Accrue* generally has a positive connotation; money in the bank *accrues* interest. *Incur* generally has a negative connotation; you *incur* liabilities, expenses, or losses: "Sportco's failure to perform the contract caused Chen to *incur* [not *accrue*] losses of over a million dollars."

admission, admittance Under the Federal Rules of Evidence, an *admission* is any statement made by a party, whether it helps or hurts. *Admittance* relates only to entering.

affect, effect These two words are frequently confused. *Affect* is most commonly used as a verb meaning "to influence":

Example 40
The statute will *affect* corporations formed after 1993.

Effect is most commonly used as a noun meaning "result" or "the condition of being in force":

Example 41
The statute will have a harmful *effect* on corporations.

Example 42
The statute does not take *effect* until 1993.

allude, refer To *allude* to something is to *refer* to it indirectly without naming it.

and, & Use the word *and*, not the symbol *&*, unless the *&* is part of the name of a business or professional organization.

and/or Avoid this construction. Purists don't like it, it's ugly, and it can be ambiguous. Almost always, either *and* or *or* alone will do the job. If you're paranoid about being misunderstood, you can use the construction "A or B or both," which is used in most statutes concerning the punishment for a crime:

Example 43
A misdemeanor is punishable by a fine of up to $700 or 90 days in jail or both.

But Example 43 could be shortened to "A misdemeanor is punishable by a fine of up to $700 and 90 days in jail" without any resultant ambiguity. The *and* in this context includes the possibility of *or*. Only if the statute said "A misdemeanor shall be punished by a fine of $700 and 90 days in jail" would it be understood to require both the fine and the jail sentence. You'll find *and* or *or* alone will similarly handle almost every other instance when you thought you needed *and/or*.

apply You *apply* rules to facts, not the other way around.

arguable, arguably When these words are used to refer to an issue, they mean it is one on which reasonable people could differ. Thus, an *arguable* position is not a strong position but merely a position an advocate could argue with a straight face. These words are also often used to refer to an issue that is moot:

Example 44
Although Garcia was *arguably* negligent, the statute of limitations has run.

assure, ensure, insure To *assure* is to promise:

Example 45
The defendant's lawyer *assured* the court her client would be present at the hearing.

To *ensure* or *insure* is to make sure something happens:

Example 46
To *ensure* [or *insure*] the defendant's appearance at the hearing, the court ordered bail set at $100,000.

because   Causation is critical in legal analysis and writing. *Because* expresses causation most directly and unambiguously. *Since* is slightly weaker because of its connotation of time. *As* is a poor substitute; its meanings of "while" or "when" make it easily ambiguous: "The court enjoined the demonstration *as* the demonstrators entered private property." *For* is also a poor substitute; readers expect it to be used as a preposition. *Inasmuch as, in that, in light of, being that, due to the fact that,* and *in view of the fact that* are all weaker and wordier than *because*.

"The reason . . . is because" is redundant; it should be "The reason . . . is that." "The reason why" is also redundant. Both redundancies are used *incorrectly* in the following example:

Example 47
The reason why the statute does not apply *is because* a skateboard is not a motor vehicle.

With the redundancies removed, the sentence is:

Example 48
The reason the statute does not apply *is that* a skateboard is not a motor vehicle.

But the sentence is even better with a simple *because*:

Example 49
The statute does not apply *because* a skateboard is not a motor vehicle.

car Police officers, out of a misguided notion that plain English is inappropriate in formal settings, are notorious for testifying that they "exited the vehicle."   If it's a car, call it a *car*, not an *automobile* or a *vehicle*. In plain English, people *get out of* cars, they don't *exit* them.

clearly *Clearly* is often an illegitimate substitute for analysis or argument.   The same is true for its one-word equivalents (*certainly, obviously, surely, patently, manifestly*, etc.) and word-wasting equivalents (*it is clear that, it is obvious that*, etc.). *Abundantly clear* compounds the problem. Instead of saying *it is clear,* just make it clear.

communication Avoid using *communication* as a vague substitute for the specific form of communication involved:

> **Example 50**
> Reese then received a *communication* from Lim complaining that the goods were defective.

Instead, be specific:

> **Example 51**
> Reese then received a letter from Lim complaining that the goods were defective.

contact Avoid using the verb *contact* as a vague substitute for a specific verb when you know what happened:

> **Example 52**
> Lim then *contacted* Reese and complained that the goods were defective.

Instead, be specific:

> **Example 53**
> Lim then *wrote* to Reese and complained that the goods were defective.

criteria, criterion *Criteria* is plural; *criterion* is singular:

> **Example 54**
> The court articulated three *criteria* for determining a person's competence to contract. The first *criterion* was whether the person understood the nature of the transaction.

desires, wants *Desires* as a verb connotes a deep longing or craving for something like sex or Haagen-Dazs. Don't use it as a verb when all you mean is *wants*, especially when you're talking about a corporation or other non-human entity.

dicta, dictum *Dicta* is the plural of *dictum*, which is a peripheral point or remark made by a court in a written opinion. Since *dicta* is a plural noun, it must be followed by a plural verb:

> **Example 55**
> The court's *dicta* in <u>Florenzano</u> *have* no effect on the traditional rule of fraud in this state.

Dictum usually doesn't take an article:

> **Example 56**
> The court's statement in <u>Hill</u> quoted by Appellant is *dictum* [not *a dictum*].

disinterested *Disinterested* means "impartial, unbiased." It is often mistakenly used to mean "uninterested." The *disinterested* judge listens with an open mind to both sides; the uninterested judge doesn't listen.

facility Don't call every kind of building a *facility*. Use a specific noun: hospital, school, plant, prison, etc.

fired In plain English, a person is *fired* from a job. To say the person was *terminated* sounds like Arnold Schwarzenegger was involved. *Discharged* is less ominous but faintly military. When you're tracking a rule or statute that talks about "wrongful termination" or "wrongful discharge," use those terms. Otherwise use *fired*, especially in your Statement of Facts. If you're talking about something other than a human being—such as a contract—then *terminate* is fine.

first, firstly To enumerate points, use *first, second,* etc., instead of the clumsier *firstly, secondly,* etc. And don't start with "First of all"; it makes you sound irritated.

former, latter The main problem with this pair is that they often make the reader look back to figure out which is which. Don't break the momentum. Eliminate them by repeating the nouns or rewriting the sentence.

ground, grounds Both *ground* and *grounds* can refer to a single reason or basis: "Chen refused to perform on the *ground* that the contract was illegal," "Chen refused to perform on *grounds* that the contract was illegal."

guilty, innocent, liable *Guilty* should be used to refer to those convicted of a crime. Don't use it to refer to those found *liable* in a civil case. Don't say:

Example 57
The jury found Dr. Garrote *guilty* of malpractice.

Say:

Example 58
The jury found Dr. Garrote *liable for* malpractice.

Or say:

Example 59
The jury found Dr. Garrotte *had committed* malpractice.

In criminal law, the opposite of *guilty* is not *innocent* but rather *not guilty*. A verdict of *not guilty* means the jury believed that the prosecution did not prove guilt beyond a reasonable doubt. It does not necessarily mean the jury believed that the defendant was *innocent.*

imply, infer To *imply* is to express indirectly, to hint. To *infer* is to conclude from evidence, to deduce. The words are not interchangeable. The speaker or writer *implies,* the listener or reader *infers*:

> **Example 60**
> The court *implied* in its opinion that it might have reached a different result if the plaintiff had been a consumer instead of a commercial buyer.

> **Example 61**
> The court *inferred* from the language of the statute that the legislature intended to treat consumers and commercial buyers differently.

in question This stilted phrase is often unclear or redundant. For example, if you've been talking about different contracts, *"the contract in question"* is less clear than "the 1991 contract," "the employment contract," "the MCA contract," or whatever. If you've been talking about only one contract, "the contract *in question*" is redundant.

in terms of No phrase is more abused by educated speakers and writers than this vague, wordy, compound preposition. Misuse starts innocently enough. You try using *in terms of* one night just for kicks, perhaps at a party with a few friends. Pretty soon you're using it at school or work. Before you know it you're hooked. The lazy high of constructing sentences without thinking about how the parts relate to each other becomes irresistible. Addicts can barely make it through a sentence without grasping for *in terms of* to glue the mess together. In speech, "uh" would be a healthier choice, if it allowed time for planning a solid sentence.

There are rare occasions when you will actually be describing one thing *in terms of* another, but ninety-nine times out of a hundred *in terms of* is just a sloppy connector:

Example 62
A deposition is an effective tool *in terms of* discovery.

In terms of can be eliminated in one of two ways. It can be replaced by a short, precise preposition such as "at," "in," or "for":

Example 63
A deposition is an effective tool *for* discovery.

Or it can be eliminated entirely by rewriting the sentence:

Example 64
A deposition is an effective discovery tool.

may, might *May* and *might* cover events that could happen from the present on: "The car *may* [or *might*] explode." But only *might* is past tense. If you're talking about someone's belief in the past that an event could happen, you must use *might*: "He thought the car *might* [not *may*] explode, but it did not."
    Sometimes it is unclear whether *may* means "is permitted to" or "might": "The court *may* enforce the contract." *May not* creates the same problem: "Reese *may not* ignore the contract." Guard against these ambiguities.

monies Avoid this archaic word. *Money* will always work in its place.

moot In ordinary contexts, a *moot* question is one that is "debatable" or "open to doubt." In legal contexts, a *moot* question is one that no longer has any legal significance: "The court's decision that the defendant was not liable rendered the damages issue *moot*." This meaning is reflected in *moot court*, which is where law students argue hypothetical cases.

motion, move A litigant *moves or makes a motion* for something, like summary judgment. A litigant does not *"motion for summary judgment"*; *motion* is used only as a noun in this context. Nor does a litigant *"move the court* for summary judgment"; "court" can't be the direct object of *move.* If you want to get "court" into the sentence, you must say something like *"moved that the court* grant summary judgment."

of course *Of course* can sound condescending, especially when you're talking about technical matters: *"Of course,* assets exempted from section 1402(a) are included under section 1402(b)." Since you rarely can be sure how much your reader knows, it's best to avoid *of course.*

prove, show Facts are *proved:* "McKinsey can *prove* the light was red." Legal conclusions aren't *proved,* they're *shown:* "Sobel can *show* [not *prove*] section 2-209 was not designed to cover her situation."
 "Has proved" is preferred over "has proven": "The State has *proved* [not *proven*] Sikes was at the scene of the murder."

purchase, sale A sales transaction can be looked at two ways. From the seller's point of view, it's a *sale;* from the buyer's point of view, it's a *purchase.* In the following example, the wrong point of view is given to the buyer:

Example 65
Although Mahoney moved in on January 1, he still owed Neville $80,000 for the *sale* of the house.

Since Mahoney is the buyer, it should say he owes the money "for the *purchase* of the house."

represents Don't use *represents* when you mean "is." A senator *represents* a state in Congress, a flag *represents* a country. But there's no relationship of representation in the following example:

Example 66
Hill *represents* the first case in which the court recognized a cause of action for wrongful life.

It should be:

Example 67
Hill *is* the first case in which the court recognized a cause of action for wrongful life.

respective, respectively These are either confusing or unnecessary. In the following example, *respectively* is confusing because it makes the reader match the lawyers with the right parties:

Example 68
At trial, John Mendoza and Beverly Wong represented Costco and Rolling Soles *respectively*.

Do the work for the reader:

Example 69
At trial, John Mendoza represented Costco and Beverly Wong represented Rolling Soles.

In the following example, *respective* is a needless word:

Example 70
Both parties dismissed their *respective* claims.

Whose claims could they dismiss but their own?

said Parties and witnesses say a lot of things. The simplest way to refer to what someone said is to say he or she *said* it. A more formal substitute for *said* is *stated*. If you're going to use any other substitute for *said*, be precise. Each word listed has its own particular meaning and connotations. Don't use these words interchangeably.

> *admitted:* said something damaging to the speaker's position (although in evidence law, an *admission* technically is anything said by an opposing party).

advised: gave advice or made a recommendation ("Attorneys for Van Buskirk *advised* him to drop the suit").

alleged: said something factual that has not yet been proved ("Norwest *alleged* in its Complaint that it gave the employee handbook to all new employees").

asserted: said something forcefully or boldly ("Beck *asserted* the counterclaim was barred by the statute of limitations").

claimed: alleged a right to something ("Kozo *claimed* half of the property under his father's will") or asserted something ("Gold *claimed* he struck Rork in self-defense").

contended: stated a position in a legal argument ("The State *contended* that the line-up did not prejudice Chen's rights").

disclosed: said something that was previously kept from public knowledge for valid reasons ("Senator Andrews *disclosed* she had decided not to seek re-election because of poor health").

indicated: said or otherwise communicated something indirectly (the most often misused substitute for *said*).

informed: conveyed information or gave a formal notice to another ("Field *informed* IBM the computer was defective in a written notice dated October 6, 1989").

represented: asserted something as true, especially about something the speaker was trying to sell ("The seller *represented* to the buyer that the house had never had water in the basement").

revealed: said something that was previously concealed ("The company *revealed* it had shut down the reactor twice because of malfunctions in the cooling system").

stipulated: agreed before a court to something, such as the existence of a fact that otherwise might be disputed in a trial ("The company *stipulated* Desnick was acting within the scope of her employment") or agreed to specific terms in a contract.

testified: said something under oath in a trial or deposition (not used regarding statements made to a police officer or investigator).

Don't use the noun forms of these words (*allegation, contention, stipulation,* etc.) interchangeably either. They have the same distinct connotations as their verb forms.

Don't use *alleged, asserted, claimed,* or *contended* to refer to something you or your client has said unless you're making a procedural point, such as "Gold has properly *alleged* a fraud claim in his Complaint." These words normally imply that you think what the speaker has said is false. Use them to refer to what the other side said. The other side *alleges* things; your client *states* them.

Finally, *said* as an adjective is pure legalese: "Chen signed *said* contract on April 10, 1992." Use plain English instead: "Chen signed *the* contract."

that *That* is often a needless word; omit it when the sentence would be just as clear without it. For example, in "The witness testified *that* the light was red," *that* can be omitted with no loss of meaning. But be careful not to omit *that* when its omission momentarily leads the reader astray, as in "The judge believed the defendant violated the statute." Until "violated," things look good for the defendant, but then the reader is jerked in the opposite direction. Better: "The judge believed *that* the defendant violated the statute."

the fact that Most books on writing recommend avoiding this phrase because it's wordy. There's another reason to avoid it in legal writing. What is a "fact" is often hotly contested, so using *the fact that* may raise a distracting battle flag in a sentence where you aren't making any assertion about "the facts":

Example 71
The fact that the court gave a limiting instruction prevented the jury from being unfairly prejudiced by the evidence.

You can usually rewrite a sentence to eliminate *the fact that*:

Example 72
The court's limiting instruction prevented the jury from being unfairly prejudiced by the evidence.

The wordy *despite the fact that* can be replaced by *although*.

timely *Timely* can be an adjective:

Example 73
The defendant made a *timely* motion for a new trial.

Or it can be an adverb:

Example 74
The defendant *timely* moved for a new trial.

Timely used as an adverb, as in Example 74, may sound strange to many ears because we subconsciously expect "ly" to be added to an adjective to form the adverb, as in "slow" and "slowly." But adding "ly" would make *timelily*, which is obsolete. If *timely* as an adverb sounds strange or stilted to you, rewrite the sentence. Make *timely* function as an adjective, as in Example 73, even if it takes a few extra words. But don't add more words than necessary by using phrases such as *in a timely manner* or *in a timely fashion*.

true facts *True facts* is generally considered a redundancy, because there is no such thing as a false fact. In a lawsuit, however, each side puts forth a different version of "the facts." Since both versions of the facts cannot be true, some lawyers believe it necessary to distinguish the *true facts* (their facts) from the other side's "facts." In this process, *facts* standing alone is devalued to mean nothing more than "alleged facts." In another fifty years, *true facts* will probably become similarly devalued from loose usage, so we'll all have to start referring to "the really true facts" to make our point. Better to hold the line at *facts* without any modifier.

whether   *Whether* seems to attract needless words. In the phrase *whether or not* you can usually omit the *or not:*

> **Example 75**
> Jurisdiction depends on *whether* [not *whether or not*] the accident occurred within the state.

The phrase *the issue as to whether* should be shortened to *the issue whether.* Similar phrases such as *the question as to whether* should be similarly shortened.

widget   All through my first-year contracts class I wondered what a *widget* was. They were bought and sold in every hypothetical. Not being mechanically inclined, I assumed it was a part used in a machine. A few years later, I looked up *widget* and found out it's not a real thing. It's a thingamajig, a whatchamacallit. Am I the only one who didn't know that?

with respect to   Avoid this vague, wordy phrase. Lawyers use it a lot when writing to a court, possibly because they believe that dotting their arguments with "respect" will evoke a subconsciously favorable response from the judge:

> **Example 76**
> The court's finding *with respect to* intent should be reversed.

Like its cousin *in terms of, with respect to* can often be replaced by a short, one-word preposition:

> **Example 77**
> The court's finding *on* intent should be reversed.

It also can often be eliminated entirely by rewriting the sentence.

Example 78
With respect to my feelings for you, I have experienced ones of a loving nature.

becomes:

Example 79
I love you.

5 Spelling

This chapter contains words that are often misspelled in legal writing. A spellchecking program will catch some of them. But if you use the wrong word from one of the pairs below that sound or look alike, the program won't catch it. And there will be times when you won't be able to use a spellchecking program, like when you're taking an exam. So spend a few minutes going through this list.

admissible, permissible, reversible All three end in "ible." I learned to spell *admissible* when I did a LEXIS search with it misspelled as "admiss<u>able</u>" and a message appeared on the screen that LEXIS had found no documents. My misspelling was understandable because I thought of *admissible* as meaning "<u>able</u> to be admitted." But good logic isn't always good spelling.

advice, advise *Advice* is the noun: "Get the *advice* of a lawyer before you sign a contract." *Advise* is the verb: "Lawyers who handle drunk-driving cases sometimes *advise* their clients to refuse to take a breath test."

alleged You will often use *alleged* as an adjective or verb to refer to something the other side said: "the *alleged* violation," "Sobel *alleged* the computer did not work," etc. *Allege* does not have a "d" like "knowledge." Since the person *alleging* is—according to you—without knowledge of the facts, this difference should remind you to spell the two words differently.

appealed The past tense of *appeal* has only one "l."

argument The "e" at the end of "argue" disappears to avoid getting caught in the middle of an *argument.*

capital, capitol *Capitol* is a building in which a state or national government meets. The "o" should remind you of the *capitol's* dome. *Capital* is everything else, including the city in which the *capitol* is located. In legal writing, *capital* is used often as a noun referring to money or other assets: "A corporation must be started with adequate *capital.*" It is also used often in legal writing as an adjective meaning "involving death or carrying the death penalty": "*capital* punishment," "a *capital* offense."

causal, casual *Causal* means "relating to causation or a cause": "There must be a *causal* connection between the defendant's negligence and the plaintiff's injury." Be careful not to reverse the "u" and the "s" in *causal* so you unintentionally write *casual.*

comparative Although "*comparative* negligence," "*comparative* fault," and "*comparative* law" involve "comparisons," an "a"— not an "i"—follows the "r" in *comparative.*

council, counsel A *council* is a governing body, as in "city council." *Counsel* as a noun refers to a lawyer or lawyers: "the right to *counsel,*" "Will *counsel* please approach the bench?" *Counsel* as a verb refers to what lawyers do for their clients.

complement, compliment To *complement* is to complete: "The regulations *complement* the statute." When someone flatters me with a *compliment*, "i" feel good.

defendant, respondent Unlike "independent," *defendant* ends in "ant." A *defendant* is no longer totally independent, because a *defendant* must answer criminal charges or a civil complaint. Maybe that difference will help you remember that the words end differently. If that doesn't work, picture a big ant on the nose of a criminal *defend<u>ant</u>*.

   Respondent is used in some states instead of *appellee*. *Respondent* is also used for the party opposing a *petitioner*. Unlike *defendant*, it ends in "ent."

exercise Rights and options are *exercised*. *Exercise* ends with "ise." Many of you *exercise* to increase the s<u>ize</u> of your muscles, which may be why you are mistakenly ending the word with "ize."

forbear, forebear A *forebear* is an ancestor. In contract law, to *forbear* is to refrain—usually from collecting a debt or suing. Refrain from inserting that extra "e" when you mean "refrain."

foreseeability For the plaintiff to recover, the injury or damages must have been *foreseeable*. When something is *f<u>ore</u>seeable*, you can see it be<u>fore</u> it happens.

indictment Although it sounds like "ind<u>i</u>t<u>e</u>ment," it's not spelled that way.

its, it's *Its* is a possessive pronoun: "The court gave three reasons for *its* decision." *It's* is a contraction for "it is." You won't be using *it's* because contractions are inappropriate in formal legal writing.

judgment In legal writing, *judgment* has no "e" after the "g."

lead, led The past tense of "read" is "read," but the past tense of *lead* is *led*. Only when you refer to the metal Superman can't see through does *lead* sound like *led*.

liable, libel One who is *liable* must pay civil damages. *Libel* is a form of defamation done in writing.

loose, lose   As a lawyer, you may *lose* a case. Luckily, it's the client who must pay the judgment or go to jail. *Loose* rhymes with "goose" and means "not tight."

merchantability   *Merchantability* is easy to spell if you think of it as a combination of two words: "merchant" and "ability." If you have ability as a merchant, you sell *merchantable* goods.

occasion, occurrence, omission   These are best learned as a group so you can see the differences in the doubling of consonants.   In *occasion,* the first consonant is doubled but the second is not.   In *omission,* the second is doubled but the first is not.   In *occurrence*—and *occurred*—both are doubled.

paid   This is a very important word to most lawyers and their clients. *Paid* is the past tense of "pay." Don't let the existence of "payee," "payor," or "note payable" lull you into changing the spelling to "payed."

parol, parole   *Parol* is an adjective meaning "oral," as in the "*parol* evidence rule."   When prisoners are put on *parole,* they are released under supervision.

personal, personnel   *Personal* means "private."   *Personnel* means "employees."

plead, pleaded   The preferred past tense of "plead" (rhymes with "seed") is *pleaded*: "The defendant *pleaded* guilty." You can say "The defendant *plead* guilty," but don't spell it *pled*.

principal, principle   *Principle* functions only as a noun, and it means "a rule."   You should be able to remember the spelling because both *principle* and "rule" end in "le."   *Principal* is everything else. It can be an adjective meaning "main." It can be a noun meaning "one who acts through an agent." It can also be a noun referring to money, particularly the amount of a debt. Finally, it can be a noun meaning "the head of a school," which everyone is supposed to remember through the unrealistic maxim that the *principal* tries to be your "pal."

privilege   The vowels are balanced: two "i's" in the first half, two "e's" in the second.

rational, rationale   *Rational* means "reasonable." *Rationale,* with an "e" on the end, is a noun that means "reasoning," as in "The *rationale* behind the court's decision."

receive   If you need to, repeat the little rhyme you learned as a kid: " 'I' before 'e' except after 'c.' "

rescission   When you *rescind* a contract, you cancel it, and the result is a *rescission.*   Picture a big <u>sci</u>ssors cutting up the contract so you'll remember the "sci" in *re<u>sci</u>ssion.*

subpoena   I can't help you here.   Just stare at this one until you memorize it.

supersede   Later laws or agreements may *supersede* earlier ones. *Supersede* ends in "sede." Most mistakes come from the natural tendency to end *supersede* like "pre<u>cede</u>" because both relate to time.

tenant, tenet   A *tenant* pays rent to a landlord. A *tenet* is a doctrine or principle: "Individual responsibility is a basic *tenet* of tort law."

therefor, therefore   The *therefore* you want to use has an "e" at the end and means "for that reason, consequently." *Therefor* without an "e" at the end means "for that," but since the word is legalese, you won't be using it.

threshold   Courts commonly refer to a *threshold* question: a question that logically must be answered first or at the outset. In one acceptable pronunciation of *threshold*, the "h" is sounded twice, so the word sounds like "thresh-hold." But although you may say the "h" twice, you should only write it once in *threshold*.

trespass   There's one "s" in "tres" and two in "pass."

v., vs.   Although *vs.* is a correct abbreviation of "versus," the convention in legal writing is to abbreviate "versus" as *v.* in case names.

who's, whose   *Who's* is a contraction for "who is." Since contractions are inappropriate in formal legal writing, you won't be using it. *Whose* is a possessive pronoun: "The woman *whose* car was stolen identified the thief."

6 Case Briefs

Case briefs are summaries you write of cases you've read. They are a study tool to help you prepare for classes and exams. They arc often the first thing you learn to write in law school. This chapter offers a few practical tips on how to approach them.

There are four basic sections in a case brief. Different texts give different formats. All include at least the following sections:

1. Facts
2. Issue
3. Holding
4. Rationale

In your Facts section, reduce the facts to the bare essentials. Just say there was a car accident; don't tell the color and make of the cars involved.

The Issue and Holding sections are paired; the holding is the court's answer to the legal issue presented by the case. When a case contains more than one issue and holding, just add an "s" to the headings.

"Rationale" is sometimes called "Reasoning" or "Analysis." In this section you should summarize what the court said about why it reached its holding. Don't stop at the surface of the case. Dig for the deepest reasons you can find.

Many formats for case briefs include additional sections such as "Procedural Posture," "Decision," "Plaintiff's Arguments," and "Defendant's Arguments." Generally you don't need them, but you can include them whenever they would be helpful. Or you can include the information that belongs in them in other sections. For example, the procedural posture could be put in your Facts section when it's relevant.

Here's an example of a case brief containing the four basic sections. It summarizes a case that took up four pages in a casebook. "D" stands for "defendant" and "P" for "plaintiff":

Example 80

Swanson v. Martin

Facts: D landowner put spring-gun in his vineyard to prevent theft. P was injured by the gun while trying to steal grapes.

Issue: May deadly force be used to protect property other than a dwelling?

Holding: No.

Rationale: Human life more valuable than property.

Case briefs are for your eyes only. The case briefs you write are for your own use and no one else's. They aren't going to be graded. Write them in whatever way works for you. Don't worry about writing complete sentences. Abbreviate whenever possible. Use any symbols you want. Do your own thing.

For exams and research, case briefs will be shorter than for classes. They will also vary from class to class. One professor may insist that you be able to explain the procedural posture of every case, so you'll always include it in your case briefs for that class. Other professors will ignore the procedural posture unless it's important for understanding a case, so you'll often omit it in your case briefs for those classes. Tailor your case briefs to meet your needs.

Your case briefs will get briefer as you gain experience. Make your case briefs long enough to contain all the information you need, but no longer. If your case briefs are almost as long as the cases they summarize, you won't have saved yourself much time when you review your notes. Besides, you couldn't possibly do a two-page case brief on every case you need to read in law school and still have time for other things in life like basic grooming.

When you start writing case briefs, they may be long because you will be just beginning to understand how to analyze cases. As your ability to recognize what is relevant in cases improves, your briefs will gradually shrink. After a year, they'll probably be no longer than half a page.

Most lawyers don't write case briefs. They jot down whatever notes they need about a case they've researched. Sometimes they'll jot down only a holding, sometimes just a few facts. Other times they'll photocopy a case and underline or highlight whatever is important to them. Like you—usually even more than you—they are limited by time. But when you're new to the law, case briefs are an effective tool to help you analyze cases and organize your notes.

Diagram or illustrate complex cases. Modern litigation is often complex. Several parties may be involved in a case, they may have complicated relationships, and they may have brought a bewildering array of claims, cross-claims, and counterclaims. Diagram the relationships and claims while you're reading the case for the first time. That will help you keep them straight as you go through the case, and the diagram will serve as a quick reference later.

You can also add illustrations to make a case more vivid and memorable. For example, for a car accident case, you could draw two cars running into each other. Put the plaintiff's name in one car and the defendant's in the other. If the plaintiff sued the manufacturer of one of the cars, draw an arrow from the plaintiff to a little factory with the manufacturer's name on it. You can make these drawings while daydreaming in class, as a productive alternative to aimless doodling.

Courts rarely follow case brief format in their opinions. Life for law students and lawyers would be much easier if courts would write their opinions in case-brief format. But the only thing you can count on is finding the facts near the front of an opinion. The issue, holding, and rationale can appear anywhere. Sometimes one of these will be missing entirely or stated unclearly. Then you must infer it from other evidence in the court's opinion. Writing a case brief isn't simply a matter of copying what a court has said. It requires analysis.

Simplify your case briefs by omitting the issue and implying it in the holding. The issue and holding in the case brief in Example 80 appeared as follows:

Example 81
Issue: May deadly force be used to protect property other than a dwelling?
Holding: No.

This can be shortened and simplified by omitting the Issue section and putting all the information in the Holding section:

Example 82
Holding: Deadly force may not be used to protect property other than a dwelling.

Now the issue is implied in the holding. Just remember that you have to be prepared to quickly translate your holding into an issue when you're called on in class.

If you decide to use both an Issue and a Holding section, at least keep the holding to a simple yes or no. Writing a holding that restates the issue in affirmative form is unnecessary, as in the following example:

Example 83
Issue: May deadly force be used to protect property other than a dwelling?
Holding: Deadly force may not be used to protect property other than a dwelling.

Avoid this duplication.

Courts and lawyers often blur the distinction between holdings and rules. If you have trouble distinguishing between a holding and a rule, it's not your fault. Courts and lawyers have been inconsistent in their use of these terms. Their inconsistency has contributed to your confusion.

Technically, a holding is more narrow than a rule. It is the result a court reaches by applying the law to the facts of a particular case. Thus, a court might hold that a contract was unconscionable or that a trial judge correctly instructed the jury on the definition of negligence.

A rule is broader. It is the principle a case stands for when applied to later cases. Thus, a court in reaching its holding might apply the rule that a contract is unconscionable when its terms surprise one party and completely favor the other party.

If I gave the technical holding of <u>Swanson v. Martin</u> using these definitions, my previous holding would become the rule:

Example 84

Holding: The trial court incorrectly instructed the jury that a property owner owed no duty of care to trespassers.

Rule: Deadly force may not be used to protect property other than a dwelling.

This is what your case briefs would look like for a professor who required you to separate the technical holding from the rule.

But judges and lawyers rarely make this fine distinction. Courts often state a rule in the form of a holding: "We hold that a landlord may not evict a tenant for reasons that are against public policy." This is especially likely to happen when the court radically changes a rule in a single case. And the cases you read in law school are especially likely to be such cases, because they are specially selected for their importance.

Even when the court does not state its holding in such broad terms, lawyers commonly state a holding in broad terms so that it sounds like a rule. Assume the court in <u>Hill</u> held that a particular landlord could not evict a particular tenant for reasons that were against public policy. In a memo or brief, a lawyer might say: "In <u>Hill</u>, the court held that *a* landlord may not evict *a* tenant for reasons that are against public policy."

One reason lawyers state holdings like rules is that they are interested in how the next case will be affected. As a law student, you should generally do the same thing, because the technical holding of a case will rarely be of much use to you. Although the technical holding in Example 84 will help you understand <u>Swanson,</u> it won't help you when you apply <u>Swanson</u> to the next case. That next case will be the professor's hypothetical in class or the situation you must analyze on an exam.

What will be of use to you appears now under the Rule heading in Example 84. That's what you need to retain, whether you call it a rule or a holding. I'd call it the holding and scrap the technical holding in Example 84. This would be my case brief of <u>Swanson:</u>

Example 85
<u>Swanson v. Martin</u>

Facts:	D landowner put spring-gun in his vineyard to prevent theft. P was injured by the gun while trying to steal grapes.
Holding:	Deadly force may not be used to protect property other than a dwelling.
Rationale:	Human life more valuable than property.

If I were really pressed for time, I'd just scribble down the holding and head for class.

7 Cases and Courts

Refer to your case unambiguously. *This case* is the simplest way to refer to your case. But be careful; it's easily ambiguous. It can be unclear whether *this case* refers to your case or to some case you recently cited as authority. There's even more potential for ambiguity when you say *in this case* or *in that case* when you mean "in that event" or "in that instance." Don't do it. If you use *this case,* use it only to refer to your case and use case names to refer to cited cases.

Another simple way to refer to your case is to say *here:*

Example 86
In <u>Kelynack</u>, the buyer had to wait three months before his motorcycle was repaired. <u>Id.</u> at 488. *Here* Field only had to wait a month to have her computer repaired.

But *here* has the same potential for ambiguity as *this case.* Be careful using it.

Other ways to refer to your case are (1) *the present case,* (2) *the current case,* (3) *the instant case,* (4) *the case at hand,* and (5) *the case at bar.* These are unambiguous, but they are also wordier than *this case* or *here.* And to some *the case at bar* sounds like a stuffy legalism and *the instant case* sounds silly because it reminds them of instant coffee. If you use any of these five phrases, at least be consistent. Don't refer to your case in one paragraph as *the current case* and in the next paragraph as *the present case.*

Our case is a natural way to refer to your case in an office memo. But you can't use it in a memo or brief to a court because first-person pronouns are inappropriate there. Another alternative in an office memo is to label the case with your client's name. Thus if your client's name is "Field" you could refer to "Field's case."

You can use "Field's case" in an office memo even if what you're referring to has not yet technically become a litigated "case," as long as it's clear you mean the potential case your client may be involved in. The same is true for other expressions with "case" except *the case at bar,* which is appropriately used only when you are addressing a court regarding the case you're litigating.

However, even if your client Field is already in a lawsuit with IBM, don't say "In <u>Field</u>" or "In <u>Field v. IBM</u>." Underlined short forms of case names are used only to refer to other cases you're citing.

If your client is not yet involved in a lawsuit, and you don't want to use the word "case" at all, you can refer to your client's *situation* or the like.

Refer to decided cases efficiently. After you've given the full citation of a decided case, you generally should refer to it in your text by only the name, or an abbreviated name, of the first party to that case. For example, after you've given the full citation for <u>Fruth v. Gaston</u>, you then can say "In <u>Fruth</u>, the court established a new rule." Don't say "In the <u>Fruth</u> case" or "In the case of <u>Fruth</u>." Omit those needless words.

Don't refer to a case by the name of the first party if that party's name is not distinctive, such as when the first party is a unit of government like "State" or "United States" or when the first party is a person identified by a governmental role like "Commissioner of Revenue." Refer to those cases by the name of the party on the other side of the "v." For example, you'd refer to "<u>State v. Hill</u>" as "<u>Hill</u>."

You can refer to a court by the name of a case it decided, as in "the <u>Hill</u> court." But this device is most aptly used when you are distinguishing one court from another or distinguishing two different compositions of the same court.

The court is "it." Even if a court has more than one judge, it is still a single entity. You should therefore use singular pronouns when referring to any court: *it* not *they*, *its* not *their*. For example:

> **Example 87**
> The court followed this rule when *it* [not *they*] decided a similar case two years later.

In a brief to an appellate court, it's usually best to refer to the trial judge impersonally as *the trial court* or *the court*. When you do that, use the gender-neutral pronouns *it* and *its*, even though you're really referring to a particular man or woman:

> **Example 88**
> *The trial court* correctly stated the rule in *its* [not *his* or *her*] instructions to the jury.

You can also refer to the judge by name or simply as "the trial judge." Use a name if the judge is particularly well-respected and you're arguing the judge did the right thing. Don't use a name if you're criticizing what the trial judge did. It may seem to the appellate court like a personal attack, and judges like to protect one another.

In a memo to a trial court, always refer to the judge as *the Court* or *this Court* rather than as *Your Honor* or *you*. Also avoid *your* in a memo to the trial court; use *the Court's, this Court's,* or *its:*

> **Example 89**
> *The Court* [not *Your Honor* or *You*] correctly stated the rule in *its* [not *your*] instructions to the jury.

Make it clear which court you're talking about. If you refer only to "the court" when talking about a cited case, readers will assume you mean the court that wrote the opinion you're citing. But although readers can figure out which court that is from the citation, telling them the name saves them work. So it's a good idea to name the court in full the first time you refer to it in connection with a case.   After that, you can switch to "the court":

Example 90
The *Texas Supreme Court* first recognized the defense of necessity in <u>Wayne v. Derek</u>, 98 S.W. 809 (Tex. 1913). *The court* held . . . .

Giving the full name of a court the first time you mention it is especially important when you're discussing cases decided by different courts.   It helps readers keep them straight.   And if one case was decided by the highest court in the jurisdiction and another by a trial court or a court outside the jurisdiction, telling the names of the courts emphasizes the difference in precedential weight between the cases.   Remember: All courts are not created equal.

If all the cases you're discussing were decided by the same court, after you name it in connection with the first case you don't have to name it in full again.

If you want to talk about a court other than the court that decided a case, you must specify it.   For example, if a state court of appeals wrote the opinion and you want to talk about what the trial court did, say it was the trial court:

Example 91
In <u>Hill</u>, *the trial court* [not *the court*] excluded the evidence as hearsay.

After giving the full name of a court, you can refer to it by a short form of its name.   For example, you could refer to the Michigan Court of Appeals as "the court of appeals."   Use an appellate court's full name or a short form if you switch back to talking about what it did in a case after talking about what the trial court did:

Example 92
In <u>Hill</u>, *the trial court* excluded the evidence as hearsay. *The court of appeals* [not *the court*] held this was harmless error.

Even though the court of appeals decided the case in Example 92, calling it simply "the court" after talking about the trial court would be ambiguous.

Avoid the phrase "the lower court." It can be ambiguous when there is more than one court below the court that wrote the opinion you're citing or more than one court below the court you're addressing. "Lower" may also seem disparaging to appellate judges who used to be on "the lower court" or who have friends currently on it. Be specific: "the district court," "the trial court," "the court of appeals," etc.

Remember which court you're talking to. Your appellate brief assignment may involve a made-up case, but the case may be set in a real jurisdiction. If it is, keep that in mind when you write your brief. If you are writing to the California Supreme Court, and you're describing the Hill case decided by the California Supreme Court, don't say "In Hill, *the California Supreme Court* established a new rule." Since you're writing to the same court that decided the case, you must say "In Hill, *this Court* established a new rule." Treat made-up cases as if they were real.

Be precise in describing what a court did. Here are the precise words for several things courts do:

grant or *deny* a motion
sustain or *overrule* an objection to evidence
accept or *reject* an argument
hold on an issue of law
find on an issue of fact
rule on an objection to evidence, motion, or issue of law
affirm, reverse (or *overturn*), or *modify* a judgment or order of a lower court
vacate (or *set aside*) a judgment or order of a lower court
remand a case to a trial court
overrule precedent

Uphold can be used synonymously for *affirm* in reference to the decision of a lower court: "The court *upheld* [or *affirmed*] the defendant's conviction." But courts *uphold*—not *affirm*—statutes, precedents, rules, rights, limitations, powers, etc.: "The court *upheld* [not *affirmed*] the limitation on the Commissioner's power." Use *affirm* only in reference to what an appellate court does to the decision of a lower court.

A court or judge writes a *memorandum* or *opinion* to explain an *order*, *judgment*, or *decision*. Sometimes a court will even *establish*, *enunciate*, or *articulate* a new rule. Juries, not judges, *return* or *hand down* verdicts.

You can say "The court *stated*" to introduce a statement the court made, but only if no more precise word applies. If the statement is a holding, say "The court *held*." If it's a finding, say "The court *found*." If it's a definition, say "The court *defined*." Be as precise as you can be.

Courts don't have feelings. Judges are human beings like the rest of us, whose decisions are often influenced by their emotions. But in our system of justice, judges are supposed to put their emotions aside and decide cases by dispassionately applying the law to the facts. That's why you shouldn't say the court *felt* something if you want that something to support your argument. Unless the court itself said it *felt* something, say the court *noted*, *thought*, *believed*, or *recognized* something.

You rarely need to give the name of the judge who wrote an opinion. In case citations, you never need to give the name of the judge who wrote an opinion unless you're citing a concurring or dissenting opinion. And you should beware of giving a judge's name in your discussion of a cited case. Referring to what Judge Nosebleed said in Hill just makes you look silly if no one has ever heard of Judge Nosebleed. Even if the judge is famous, and you think giving the judge's name will add precedential weight to the case, giving it is risky when writing to a court. Strong cases stand on their own. Your use of the judge's name may be taken as a tacit admission you're insecure about the rule you're citing the case for. Or the court you're writing to may not like the particular judge you've named. Or the court may think you pretentious for giving the name, as if you were trying to imply that you and Learned Hand hung out together. So avoid name-dropping when discussing cases.

Use the past tense to describe everything about a case except the rule. The tendency to use the present tense when talking about cases arises understandably because a court's opinion—if it's still good law—is a living document. Its words, even if written long ago, still control the lives of citizens and the fate of litigants. Nevertheless, talk in the past tense about a court's saying or doing something:

> **Example 93**
> In Kelynack, the court *stated* [not *states*] that it might have reached a different result had the plaintiff been a commercial buyer rather than a consumer.

Note that it is the court in Example 90 that "stated," not the case. Don't say "Kelynack stated."

Also talk about the facts of a case in the past tense:

> **Example 94**
> In Hill, a pit bull *bit* [not *bites*] a child.

On the other hand, express the rule from a case in the present tense:

> **Example 95**
> In Hill, the court held that an owner of a dangerous animal *is* [not *was*] strictly liable for injuries caused by the animal.

Only if the rule in Example 95 were no longer good law would you use the past tense.

Also use the present tense to talk about statutes currently in force:

Example 96
Section 2-719(2) *provides* [not *provided*] that if a limited remedy fails of its essential purpose, the buyer can resort to other remedies.

Only if the statute has been repealed or modified would you use the past tense. And omit a needless word by saying "*under* section 2-719(2)" instead of "*pursuant to* section 2-719(2)."

Compare apples with apples when comparing cases. Make sure you're not comparing apples with oranges:

Example 97
Like <u>Hill</u>, Wold was arrested without a warrant.

In Example 97, a case ("<u>Hill</u>") has been compared to a person ("Wold"). This is called a "false comparison." Compare apples with apples:

Example 98
Like the defendant in <u>Hill</u>, Wold was arrested without a warrant.

Example 99
Like <u>Hill</u>, this case involves a warrantless arrest.

If you want to compare your case to a cited case without comparing two matching nouns, instead of *like* or *like in* you must use *as in*:

Example 100
In <u>Hill</u>, *as in* [not *like* or *like in*] this case, the defendant was arrested without a warrant.

Cases aren't distinguished until you distinguish them. You can't say case A *is distinguished* from case B. The cases are merely *distinguishable* until you actually *distinguish* them. So say case A *is distinguishable* or *can be distinguished* from case B, and then go on to distinguish it. If a court has already distinguished the case for you, then you can say case A *was distinguished* from case B by that court.

Cases are always distinguishable on countless facts, but only some of the distinctions have significance. Just because the plaintiff's last name in a cited case began with a vowel and your client's last name begins with a consonant doesn't mean the result in your case should be different. Explain the significance of any distinction you make. Rely only on differences that make a difference.

8 Names

Refer to the parties in your case by their names unless their litigation roles are more persuasive. Using the names of parties is almost always the clearest way to refer to them. Many lawyers use names in an office memo, but switch to litigation roles when writing to a court, perhaps out of some mistaken sense that names aren't formal enough for such formal documents. Yet no rule requires this switch.

Generally stick with names when writing to a court. It's easy to forget who is "Appellant" or "Plaintiff," much less "Defendant/Respondent." You've probably read countless cases where halfway through you've had to turn back to the beginning to straighten out the parties when they were referred to that way. The same thing happens to a judge reading a memorandum or brief. Using names prevents this confusion and helps make the facts of your case more vivid. When your client is a person (as opposed to a corporation or other entity) using a name also humanizes the client.

You don't need to use litigation roles even in the more formal sections of a memorandum or brief, such as in the Statement of the Case or Conclusion. Once you've introduced the parties and explained their roles, refer to them by their names right through to the end.

Only use litigation roles for the parties when it fits your strategy. Roles are abstractions, and abstractions don't arouse emotions the way names do. Use roles for both sides when the opposing party's name will arouse the sympathy of the court. If your client ran over Mother Teresa, go with *Plaintiff* and *Defendant*. Also use roles for both sides whenever you fear your client's name will arouse the prejudices of the court. Call Saddam Hussein *Appellant*.

Don't try to have it both ways by referring to your client by name and the opposing party by role unless there's a logical reason for doing so. To preserve your credibililty, you must always attempt to appear evenhanded. Usually that means you must choose between using names for both sides or roles for both sides.

Pick a clear and persuasive name for a business or the government. When you represent a business, you may have some discretion in picking the name to use for it. For cxample, if your client's name is "Ma's Cookies Consolidated, Inc.," you could refer to it as "Ma's Cookies" for short. This makes the corporation seem smaller and more human. Using "MCCI" wouldn't accomplish this result.

But you may have no choice about how to refer to a business client. "MCCI" may be the name everyone knows the company by, or the name all the witnesses referred to the company by, or the name for the company in all the exhibits in the case. In those situations, using any other name might create confusion and cause the court to resent your manipulation of the name.

You can also use naming strategy when the opposing party is a business. In one case I worked on, the other side was a small subsidiary of Sinclair Oil called "Sinclair Marketing, Inc." In its brief, its lawyer referred to it as "SMI." In my brief, I referred to it as "Sinclair." I hoped by calling it that to remind the appellate court that this subsidiary was really part of a huge oil company that could easily afford to pay the damages awarded to my client in the trial court.

If your client is a unit of government, the best choice is usually "the City," "the County," "the State," or the like. Lawyers for the federal government prefer "the United States." "The United States of America" has a nice patriotic ring, but it's too long and clumsy. Lawyers representing clients against the federal government prefer to call it "the Government"—a name that invokes Kafkaesque images of an ominous, monolithic authority.

Pick a clear and persuasive name for a group of litigants. If you have more than two clients in one case, it's usually too cumbersome to continually name them all. You will have to come up with a generic name for the group. Try to find something more descriptive than "Plaintiffs" or "Defendants." Referring to them by a name that reflects their role in the transaction or occurrence that led to the lawsuit (their real-life role) will make your writing easier to follow. Examples are: "the employees," "the investors," "the consumers."

If possible, choose a name for the group that fits your persuasive strategy too. For example, suppose several buyers of houses in a project are suing a corporation that developed the project and sold them the houses. The lawyer representing the buyers might want to call them "the homeowners" and the corporation "the developer" to emphasize the difference in size and power between the two sides. The lawyer representing the corporation, on the other hand, might want to call it "the seller" and the buyers "the buyers," to create the impression the parties had equal power.

When there are different but equally reasonable ways to name the parties, the battle may be won by whichever lawyer gets to name them first. The other lawyer may go along just for the sake of consistency. So choose carefully when you get the chance to name the parties first.

Introduce short-form names efficiently. When you mention a person for the first time, give the person's first and last name. After that, with no further explanation, switch to the last name alone:

Example 101
This case involves a contractual dispute between Daniel Simon and Lizette Garcia. *Simon* and *Garcia* entered into a contract in 1987 . . . .

You can use the same technique with a business or the government when it's obvious what your short form refers to. Give the full name the first time, then switch—with no explanation—to the short form:

Example 102
This case involves a contractual dispute between Hennepin County and Tirecycle Technologies, Inc. *The County* and *Tirecycle* entered into a contract in 1987 . . . .

If it's not obvious what your short form refers to, put the short form in quotation marks in a parenthetical after the full name:

Example 103
This case involves a contractual dispute between Hennepin County and Tirecycle Technologies, Inc. ("TTI"). *The County* and *TTI* entered into a contract in 1987 . . . .

Before assigning a short-form name in a parenthetical and making the reader do the work of memorizing it, make sure you're going to use it more than a few times in your document. Don't assign short-form names automatically.

To introduce your short-form name for a group of litigants you can use a complete sentence:

Example 104
Paul Stoltz, William Luther, Soo Wong, and Biagio Ciatti are referred to in this brief as "the buyers."

Or you can use a parenthetical:

Example 105
Paul Stoltz, William Luther, Soo Wong, and Biagio Ciatti ("the buyers") . . . .

You don't need *hereinafter* in your parentheticals; it's legalese and always unnecessary. Many writers fail to keep the promises they make with their *hereinafters*. Or they make lame promises to begin with: (*sometimes* referred to hereinafter as "the buyers"). You know better. Whatever short form you use for a party, stick with it.

Don't use artificial titles for people. Don't use *Mr.*, *Ms.*, *Mrs.*, or *Miss* in a memo or brief even in the full form of a person's name the first time it's mentioned. These titles just add clutter.

You don't even need *Mr.* or *Ms.* to convey the sex of a person who has an androgynous first name. Convey the person's sex by using a pronoun shortly after the full name:

Example 106
Office Terry Garwin arrived at the scene five minutes after the accident. *She* immediately blockaded the area.

Readers want to know the sex of the people involved in your case because it helps them visualize the events that occurred. It isn't sexist to satisfy this natural curiosity.

When a person's name normally includes a title, use it. "President Bush," or "Dr. Bronner," or "Commissioner Alch" are natural and correct. But don't give people titles in your writing they don't have in real life, as in the following example:

Example 107
Richard Guyett and Claudia Jackson were the only witnesses to the accident. The police interviewed *witness Guyett* one hour after the accident occurred.

"Witness Guyett" is not his title in real life. Don't use "attorney" as a title either, as in "*attorney* Snyder" or "*Attorney* Snyder."

The exception to this rule is the practice of attaching the parties' litigation roles to their names like titles: "Defendant Hackles," "Respondent Citibank." Lawyers who do this usually don't do it for long, often not past the first reference to the party. Then they'll either drop the name or the litigation role, like a water-skier dropping one ski:

Example 108
Plaintiff Citibank submits this memorandum in support of its motion for summary judgment. *Citibank* is the payee on a promissory note executed by *Defendant Hackles*. The note came due almost a year ago and *Hackles* did not pay it.

Finally, don't talk like a police officer on the witness stand. Don't say: "*A* Richard Guyett witnessed the accident" or "*One* Richard Guyett witnessed the accident." Omit the stilted *a* or *one*.

Be careful using first names alone. Referring to your client by first name alone will usually be stretching the humanizing tactic too far. It can backfire if it looks like an obvious play for sympathy.

In certain situations, however, using first names alone makes sense. Where two parties have the same last name, such as in a divorce case, it's more efficient to refer to "John" and "Mary" rather than to "Mr. Smith" and "Mrs. Smith," or "John Smith" and "Mary Smith."

Referring to a child by first name alone is natural and— when the child is your client—desirable. You can stretch the definition of "child" to include most people up to about 21. Just don't get greedy. If a boy's parents called him "Bill" on the witness stand, don't call him "Billy" in your brief.

Avoid initialese. "Initialese" refers to the overuse of words formed from initials. Initialese can make your sentences look like chemistry formulas:

Example 109
MLPF&S was an ERISA fiduciary of the PSP.

Use words as abbreviations instead of initials whenever possible. In Example 109, "MLPF&S" stands for "Merrill Lynch, Pierce,

Fenner and Smith," "ERISA" for "Employee Retirement Income Security Act," and "PSP" for "Profit Sharing Plan." "ERISA" is how that statute is commonly referred to, so it should stay the way it is. But "Merrill Lynch, Pierce, Fenner and Smith" would be better as "Merrill Lynch" and "Profit Sharing Plan" as "the plan." Then the sentence would look more like English and be easier to understand:

Example 110
Merrill Lynch was an ERISA fiduciary of *the plan.*

"The" is optional before litigation roles. If you decide to refer to a party in your case or a cited case by the party's litigation role, you can choose whether to use *the* before it:

Example 111
The accident occurred while *Plaintiff* was driving south on Elm Street.

Example 112
The accident occurred while *the Plaintiff* was driving south on Elm Street.

This rule applies to the following litigation roles: *Plaintiff, Defendant, Appellant, Appellee, Petitioner, Respondent.* It does not apply to other legal roles, such as *donor, donee, testator, executor, decedent,* etc.

I think leaving out *the* makes writing sound like headnote style, so I always put it in. Whatever you do, be consistent. At least avoid switching in the same sentence.

Refer to the parties in a cited case by their real-life roles if possible. When you talk about the facts of a case you've cited, often the best way to refer to the parties is by their real-life roles (such as "tenant" or "employer") as opposed to their litigation roles or their names. This is especially true when you're dealing with several cases involving opposing parties with equivalent roles. For example, if your issue involves the sale of goods or real estate, the cases you cite will almost all have a buyer on one side and a seller on the other. If you call the parties to each of those cases "the buyer" and "the seller," the reader will easily and quickly grasp their facts. There's no need to introduce the parties; just dive right in:

Example 113
The Third Circuit dealt with unconscionability in a commercial context in <u>Chatlos Systems v. National Cash Register Corp.</u>, 635 F.2d 1081 (3rd Cir. 1980). In <u>Chatlos</u>, *the buyer* bought a computer that broke down after only three months of use. *The seller* never successfully repaired it. <u>Id.</u> at 1084.

This method works well with many recurring sets of relationships. In corporate law, you may have several cases involving "the corporation" and "the shareholders." In labor law, it will be "the employer" and "the employee." In tax law, it will be "the IRS," "the Commissioner," or "the Government" and "the taxpayer." The list of examples could go on and on: "the landlord" and "the tenant," "the company" and "the insured," etc. Look for these relationships and use them to make your memos and briefs easier to follow.

One important exception to this rule occurs in criminal law, where defendants are usually referred to by their litigation role. When you use the litigation role of a party in a cited case, use the role in the trial court, not the role on appeal: "the defendant," not "the appellant" or "the appellee."

Refer to the parties in a cited case by their names if you're going to use more than one quotation containing their names. The more quotations containing the parties' names you use from a case, the clumsier it is to refer to the parties by their roles. You can prepare for that problem in one of several ways. You can tell who was who when you first give the facts of the case:

Example 114
In <u>Chatlos</u>, the buyer (Chatlos) bought a computer that broke down after only three months of use. The seller (NCR) never successfully repaired it.

Now your reader should be able to follow a quotation using only the parties' names:

Example 115
The court stated: "NCR repeatedly attempted to correct the deficiencies, but still had not provided the product warranted a year after Chatlos had reasonably expected a fully operational computer." Id. at 1086.

Even though in the case name the seller is called "National Cash Register Corporation," I called it "NCR" in Example 114 because that's what the court calls it in the quotation I planned to use. I used "Chatlos" for the same reason. If you use names, use the same names the court uses.

Another way to handle a quotation with names when you've been using roles is to substitute roles for names in the quotation:

Example 116
The court stated: "[The seller] repeatedly attempted to correct the deficiencies, but still had not provided the product warranted a year after [the buyer] had reasonably expected a fully operational computer." Id. at 1086.

Still another way is to add roles after the names in the quotation:

Example 117
The court stated: "NCR [the seller] repeatedly attempted to correct the deficiencies, but still had not provided the product warranted a year after Chatlos [the buyer] had reasonably expected a fully operational computer." Id. at 1086.

A final possibility is to leave the quotation as it is, if it's clear what the parties' roles were. This might have worked for the quotation in Example 117. It's fairly clear from the sentence that NCR was the seller and Chatlos the buyer. But it must be immediately clear to the reader; you can't afford to confuse the reader for even an instant.

The methods used in Examples 116 and 117 work fine if you only need to change one quotation. But if you're going to use more than one quotation with names in it, it's probably best to use names throughout your discussion of the case:

Example 118
In <u>Chatlos</u>, Chatlos bought a computer that broke down after only three months of use. NCR, the seller, never successfully repaired it. <u>Id.</u> at 1084.

If you start your description of a case using the method in Example 118 and then stick with the parties' names from then on, you won't have to keep altering quotations. Overbracketing makes a quotation hard to read.

A business or institution is "it." This is the same advice I gave regarding courts in the previous chapter. Business entities (such as corporations and partnerships) and institutions (such as universities and government agencies) take singular pronouns. For example:

Example 119
IBM makes volume discounts available to *its* [not *their*] larger customers.

Sometimes, however, a singular pronoun will sound awkward:

Example 120
Field called IBM and *it* told her the warranty on her computer had expired.

One solution to this problem is to include the individual representing the entity in the sentence:

Example 121
Field called IBM and *a customer representative* told her the warranty on her computer had expired.

Another solution—not to be overused—is to switch to the passive voice:

Example 122
Field called IBM and *was told* the warranty on her computer had expired.

Put legal arguments into the mouths of the parties, not their lawyers. We all know legal arguments are made not by the parties themselves, but by their lawyers. Nonetheless, it is traditional and efficient to speak of arguments as if they had been made by the parties. Thus, in an office memo, if you are anticipating the argument of the other side, say *"IBM* will argue," not *"Counsel for IBM* will argue." Similarly, in a brief say *"IBM* argues," not *"Counsel for IBM* argues" or *"Opposing counsel* argues."

9 Citations

Citation form is a litmus test of your credibility. Judging a writer's credibility is hard. Readers draw large inferences from small clues, and citation form is one place they look. Like spelling, citation form is either right or wrong. Especially in citations to commonly-cited sources like cases and statutes, where a reader is likely to recognize an error, your citation form should be perfect.

The *Bluebook* is still the bible of citation form. Unfortunately, it's too long, too complicated, and too picky. My *User's Guide to the Bluebook* makes mastering the rules of citation form as quick and painless as possible. This chapter covers a few of the rules that cause students particular trouble as well as a few matters of citation style the *Bluebook* neglects.

Use underlining instead of italics in citations. Use the same typeface for citations that you use in your text: ordinary roman typeface and underlining. Practitioners' note P.1 in the *Bluebook* says that italics are indicated by underlining in "word-processed or typewritten materials." That includes your memos and briefs.

Don't be thrown off by the italics and large and small capitals used in most of the *Bluebook* examples. Those examples are in the proper form for law review footnotes.

Use "sec." in citation sentences if you can't make the section symbol (§). The *Bluebook* offers no advice about what to do if your typewriter or printer can't make the section symbol (§). Students have tried all sorts of makeshift solutions: drawing it in by hand, typing one small "s" above another, substituting a dollar sign ($) or the "at" symbol (@). None of these works well.

I recommend using the abbreviation "sec." in place of the section symbol in a citation sentence (a sentence that contains only a citation):

Example 123
The statute exempts from disclosure "intra-agency memorandums." 5 U.S.C. *sec.* 552(b)(5).

If you refer to a statute in text, Rule 6.2(b) in the *Bluebook* says you have to write out the word "section" in full:

Example 124
Under *section* 552(b)(5), "intra-agency memorandums" are exempt from disclosure.

Put citations at the end of or out of your sentences. Citations break the flow of your sentences and make them hard to read:

Example 125
In <u>Tiedeman v. Morgan</u>, 435 N.W.2d 86 (Minn. Ct. App. 1992), the court interpreted the Good Samaritan Law.

One way to avoid this problem is to move the citation to the end of the sentence:

Example 126
The court interpreted the Good Samaritan Law in <u>Tiedeman v. Morgan</u>, 435 N.W.2d 86 (Minn. Ct. App. 1992).

Another way to avoid this problem is to move the citation completely out of the sentence:

Example 127
The court has recently interpreted the Good Samaritan Law. <u>Tiedeman v. Morgan</u>, 435 N.W.2d 86 (Minn. Ct. App. 1992).

Think of citation sentences as footnotes. When you cite a case in full for the first time in a citation sentence, you must be careful how you refer to it in the following textual sentence. Think of a citation sentence such as the one in Example 127 as being outside your text, like a footnote. If you refer to the case in the textual sentence following it, identify the case by its short-form name:

Example 128
The court has recently interpreted the Good Samaritan Law. <u>Tiedeman v. Morgan</u>, 435 N.W.2d 86 (Minn. Ct. App. 1992). In <u>Tiedeman</u>, a seventeen-year-old boy was at the home of his girlfriend when he became ill.

Don't immediately refer to the case using "there" or "that case," as in the following example:

Example 129
The court has recently interpreted the Good Samaritan Law. <u>Tiedeman v. Morgan</u>, 435 N.W.2d 86 (Minn. Ct. App. 1992). *In that case*, a seventeen-year-old boy was at the home of his girlfriend when he became ill.

The textual sentence following the citation sentence in Example 129 incorrectly talks about the case as if it had already been mentioned in the text.

Cite a specific page when you quote or refer to something specific in a case. Most of you know you must cite a specific page when you quote from a case. But you must also cite a specific page when you refer to something specific in a case—especially a holding or legal rule—even if you don't quote:

Example 130
The court has recently interpreted the Good Samaritan Law. <u>Tiedeman v. Morgan</u>, 435 N.W.2d 86 (Minn. Ct. App. 1992). It held that the statute supplements the common law duty to rescue. <u>Id.</u> at 89.

The second sentence of text in Example 130 is followed by a citation to a specific page ("<u>Id.</u> at 89") even though it doesn't contain a quotation.

Sometimes you will quote or refer to something specific in a case the first time you cite it. When you do that, include the citation to a specific page in the full citation. Insert the specific page number after the page number the case starts on, and separate the two with a comma:

Example 131
The court has recently held that the Good Samaritan Law supplements the common law duty to rescue. <u>Tiedeman v. Morgan</u>, 435 N.W.2d *86, 89* (Minn. Ct. App. 1992).

Notice you don't use "at" when you include the specific page in the full citation.

Once you've given a citation for something specific, you don't have to give the citation again. You must cite a specific page when you quote or refer to something specific in a case or other source, but only the first time. That first citation proves to the reader you aren't making anything up. After that, you can use the specific material you quoted or referred to any number of times without ever citing the source again.

For example, the first time you give a fact in your Statement of Facts, you will follow it with a citation to the record. Having thus proved that the fact came from the record, you can use it as many times as you want in your argument without ever citing the record again.

However, you can always choose to repeat a specific citation if the material cited is critical to your argument.

Position citations so you don't have to put one after every sentence. Although you must cite a specific page whenever you quote or refer to something specific in a case, you don't have to put a citation after every sentence. Describing a case thoroughly may take a full paragraph or more. Putting a citation after every sentence in a description that long would be awkward and distracting. Avoid this clutter by positioning your citations efficiently.

Think of a cited case as a picnic blanket. Citations are rocks you put along the edges to keep it from flapping in the wind. If you position the rocks carefully, you don't need to cover the entire edge.

You'd start by putting rocks at the four corners of the blanket. Similarly, you should always put a citation after your first statement about a case and after your last. This avoids loose ends.

Also put a citation after every quotation. You don't need a citation after every sentence when you give a holding or rule, but you shouldn't go more than two or three sentences without inserting one. And put one in when you switch from one page to another in the original.

The most logical place to omit citations is in your description of the facts of a case. If the reader wants to check the facts of a case, they're easily found at the beginning of the opinion. Your case description might therefore look something like this:

Example 132

The Minnesota Court of Appeals has recently interpreted the Good Samaritan Law. <u>Tiedeman v. Morgan</u>, 435 N.W.2d 86 (Minn. Ct. App. 1989). In <u>Tiedeman</u>, a seventeen-year-old boy was at the home of his girlfriend when he became ill. His girlfriend's parents were aware he had heart problems. Yet when his girlfriend dialed 911 for help, her father canceled the call. Her father then asked the boy whether he wanted to go to the hospital, but the boy said he felt better and did not need to go. A half hour later, the boy suffered a heart attack that caused severe brain damage. <u>Id.</u> at 87. The court held that on these facts the girlfriend's parents may have violated their statutory duty to assist the boy, and that therefore summary judgment against the boy was inappropriate. <u>Id.</u> at 89.

Note there is only one citation ("<u>Id.</u> at 87") for all the facts given and it comes at the end of the description of the facts. One rock holds this entire section of the blanket down.

There are two exceptions to this strategy of cutting corners in your citations to the facts of a case. First, if the case is long, with more than three pages of facts, help the reader by citing specific pages more often. Second, if a particular fact is crucial to your analysis or argument, by all means cite the specific page on which it can be found.

Use proper short form for case citations. The *Bluebook* gives you several options for a short-form citation to a case after you've first given the full citation. The following are acceptable short-form citations to a particular page:

> **Example 133**
> Tiedeman v. Morgan, 435 N.W.2d at 89.

> **Example 134**
> Tiedeman, 435 N.W.2d at 89.

> **Example 135**
> 435 N.W.2d at 89.

You can use *Id.* if the citation preceding it is to Tiedeman:

> **Example 136**
> Id. at 89.

But don't use *Id.* if there's any possibility of confusion about what the *Id.* refers to.

Don't use the name of a case plus a page number as a short form:

> **Example 137**
> Tiedeman at 89.

This form is not a suggested short form in the *Bluebook*.

You must give parallel citations when you cite a state case in a memo or brief to a court of the same state. If the full citation contains parallel citations, such as "Smith v. Hubbard, 253 Minn. 215, 91 N.W.2d 756 (1958)," a short form comparable to Example 135 giving parallel citations would look like this:

> **Example 138**
> 253 Minn. at 225, 91 N.W.2d at 764.

A short form comparable to Example 136 giving parallel citations would look like this:

Example 139
Id. at 225, 91 N.W.2d at 764.

Use common sense in deciding which short form to use. Never make the reader turn back to figure out what you're citing. If the name of the case appears earlier on the page, "435 N.W.2d at 89" and "Id. at 89" are fine. When you move to a new page, these may be clear if you've been talking about a single case for a long time. But if there could be any doubt, when you move to a new page use "Tiedeman, 435 N.W.2d at 89" as your first citation. Then go back to the short forms that don't include a name.

Don't use a short form that includes the name when the name appears in the preceding sentence. In the following example, the name in the citation is redundant and should be omitted:

Example 140
In Tiedeman, the court held that the statute supplements the common law duty to rescue. Tiedeman, 435 N.W.2d at 89.

Don't give a short form of a case name until after you've given the full citation. Short form names and citations must not come before the first full citation of a case. In the following example, "In Tiedeman" *incorrectly* comes first:

Example 141
In Tiedeman, the Minnesota Court of Appeals interpreted the Good Samaritan Law. Tiedeman v. Morgan, 435 N.W.2d 86 (Minn. Ct. App. 1989). It held that the statute supplements the common law duty to rescue. Id. at 89.

The short form correctly appears for the first time after the full citation in the following example:

Example 142
The Minnesota Court of Appeals has recently interpreted the Good Samaritan Law. Tiedeman v. Morgan, 435 N.W.2d 86 (Minn. Ct. App. 1989). In Tiedeman, the court held that the statute supplements the common law duty to rescue. Id. at 89.

Avoid introductory signals.   An introductory signal at the beginning of a citation—like See, e.g., Accord, Contra, Cf.—is supposed to indicate how you are using a case or other authority.   But a signal is usually too imprecise for the job.   The only consistently clear way to introduce an authority is with no signal at all.   The absence of an introductory signal means the cited authority clearly states the proposition the citation follows.   Or it can mean the cited authority is the authority you've just referred to or quoted.   If you're using a cited authority in any other way in a memo or brief, explain how in your text.

Don't put a citation after a sentence containing one of your conclusions.   When a citation follows a proposition and is not preceeded by an introductory signal, it means the cited authority clearly states the proposition.   The following example is *wrong* because the cited case says nothing about Sportco:

Example 143
Sportco can revoke the contract on the grounds of mutual mistake. Tannick v. Heins, 508 N.E.2d 889 (Ohio 1991).

Reach your conclusions step by step.   First state the legal rule in its pure form followed by the citation.   Then go on to state your conclusion in a separate sentence:

Example 144
A mutual mistake is grounds for revoking a contract. Tannick v. Heins, 508 N.E.2d 889 (Ohio 1991). Sportco can revoke its contract with Sanchez because the parties made a mutual mistake about which property was being sold.

Sometimes one of the parties is plugged into a neutral statement of the legal rule:

Example 145
If Sportco can show a mutual mistake, it can revoke the contract. <u>Tannick v. Heins</u>, 508 N.E.2d 889 (Ohio 1991).

This hybrid form is less objectionable because the implication is more modest. You're not asking the reader to believe the cited case automatically makes you a winner, only that it contains a rule that's relevant.

10 Quotations

Use as few quotations as possible. The reader expects you to analyze the law, separate the important from the unimportant, and present the law clearly and simply in your own words. Don't dump these tasks in the reader's lap by using too many quotations. Quotations also interrupt the flow of your writing and break the direct connection between you and the reader.

Quote only when the exact language in the original is important. Paraphrase whenever possible. No one can accuse you of plagiarism as long as you cite your sources.

If you don't understand the law, you'll be tempted to quote liberally in an office memo so your boss will be able to tell if you've misinterpreted something. A better solution is to find someone who can explain the law to you.

Keep quotations as short as possible. Long, single-spaced, block quotations are visually uninviting. Readers often assume their substance can be found elsewhere in your text, and therefore tend to skim or skip them. Don't strain your readers' eyes or try their patience. If you must use a quotation, zero in on the critical language and cut out the rest. If you must use a long quotation, underline the critical language to focus the attention of the reader and catch the eye of the skimmer.

Summarize the substance of long or difficult quotations. Readers expect you to summarize long or difficult quotations. Don't disappoint them. You can summarize a quotation immediately before or after it. In the following example, the sentence after the quotation summarizes it by explaining it in different terms:

Example 146
A plaintiff's contributory fault does not bar recovery "if the contributory fault was not greater than the fault of the person against whom recovery is sought." Minn. Stat. sec. 604.01, subd. 1. *Thus, if the plaintiff was more than fifty percent at fault, recovery is barred.*

Integrate quotations into your text. Quotations should fit smoothly into the flow of your text both stylistically and grammatically. Just dropping them in without integrating them gives your writing a cut-and-paste look:

Example 147
Mushki's own negligence in relying on the car dealer's misrepresentations could affect his recovery. "We hold that the principles of comparative responsibility apply to negligent misrepresentation." Florenzano v. Olson, 387 N.W.2d 168, 176 (Minn. 1986). "Without question, principles of comparative negligence would not apply to an intentional tort; we have never so applied them." Id. at 175. Therefore, if the car dealer's misrepresentations were intentional, Mushki's negligence would not affect his recovery. But if the car dealer's misrepresentations were negligent, Mushki's recovery could be reduced or barred.

The quotations in Example 147 are shoved into the paragraph like unfamiliar guests being shoved into a party by the host and abandoned. Help a quotation feel at home in your paragraph:

Example 148
Mushki's own negligence in relying on the car dealer's misrepresentations could affect his recovery. *The Minnesota Supreme Court held recently that* "the principles of comparative responsibility apply to negligent misrepresentation." Florenzano v. Olson, 387 N.W.2d 168, 176 (Minn. 1986). *But the court stated that* "without question, principles of comparative negligence would not apply to an intentional tort." Id. at 175. Therefore, if the car dealer's misrepresentations were intentional, Mushki's negligence would not affect his recovery. But if the car dealer's misrepresentations were negligent, Mushki's recovery could be reduced or barred.

If you include a quotation as part of one of your sentences, it must fit grammatically with the rest of the sentence. The quotation doesn't fit in the following example:

Example 149
Mushki stated in *his* deposition that *he* "placed *my* total reliance on the car dealer to choose a car that was mechanically sound."

In Example 149, the pronoun referring to Mushki in the quotation ("my") is in the first person, while the pronouns referring to Mushki in the rest of the sentence ("his" and "he") are in the third person. Alter the quotation or rewrite the sentence to eliminate the inconsistency:

Example 150
Mushki stated in *his* deposition that *he* "placed [*his*] total reliance on the car dealer to choose a car that was mechanically sound."

Example 151
Mushki stated in *his* deposition that *he* placed *his* "total reliance on the car dealer to choose a car that was mechanically sound."

Example 152
In his deposition, Mushki stated: "*I* placed *my* total reliance on the car dealer to choose a car that was mechanically sound."

Indent and single-space long or important quotations. Long or important quotations should be block quotations: indented left and right and single-spaced without quotation marks. Don't attach the citation to the block quotation. Put it on the next double-spaced line following the quotation and then continue with your text.

Except for block quotations, the text in your memos and briefs will be double-spaced. To save space, all the examples in this book are single-spaced. But the following example appears exactly as it would on your page, so you can see the relation between the double-spaced text and the single-spaced quotation:

Example 153
The court in <u>Florenzano</u> defined the circumstances in which fraudulent intent was present:

> Intent is present when the misrepresenter knows the matter is not as he or she represents it. Intent is also present when a misrepresenter speaks without qualification, but is conscious of ignorance of the truth, <u>or realizes the information on which he or she relies is inadequate to support such an unqualified assertion.</u>

387 N.W.2d at 173 (emphasis added). Thus, knowledge of falsity is not required for fraudulent intent.

Rule 5.1 in the *Bluebook* says quotations of forty-nine or fewer words should not be set off from the text. You should break this rule whenever you have a short quotation that's important and you want to make it stand out. Lawyers do it all the time. Also, grown-ups shouldn't have to count words. The rule should be just as I stated it: Indent and single-space long or important quotations.

Punctuate quotations correctly. Periods and commas always go inside the quotation marks. They're small so they fit:

Example 154
Mushki stated the car was "mechanically *sound,*" but in need of "minor *repairs.*"

Semicolons and colons, like skis that must go on the roof of your car, always go outside the quotation marks:

Example 155
Under section 1961(4), there are two requirements for a *"pattern"*: relatedness and continuity.

Question marks and exclamation points go inside or outside depending on whether they are part of the quotation:

Example 156
The prosecutor then asked: "When did you last see the
victim?"

Correctly show changes in quotations. When you use a quotation as a phrase or clause in one of your sentences, don't
indicate that you've omitted language or citations from the
beginning or end of the quotation:

Example 157
When the employment is at-will, "the employer can summarily
dismiss the employee for any reason or no reason." Pine
River, 333 N.W.2d at 627.

The full sentence from which I took the quotation in Example
157 read as follows: "This means that the employer can
summarily dismiss the employee for any reason or no reason,
and that the employee, on the other hand, is under no
obligation to remain on the job."
    But if you omit language from within a quotation, indicate
the omission with three periods, called an "ellipsis." Separate
the periods with spaces, and leave a space before the first period
and after the last period:

Example 158
"Where the hiring is for an indefinite term . . . the employment
is said to be at-will." Pine River, 333 N.W.2d at 627.

When you omit citations or footnotes from within a quotation,
you don't need an ellipsis. Instead, put the phrase "citations
omitted" or "footnotes omitted" in a parenthetical at the end of
your citation.
    If you use a quotation as a full sentence, then you must
indicate an omission from the beginning or end. To indicate an
omission from the beginning, change the first letter of the first
word of your quotation from lower to upper case and put it in
brackets. Never begin a quotation with an ellipsis. To indicate
an omission from the end, use four periods. Three of the
periods function as the ellipsis; one as the sentence-ending

period. Language has been omitted from both ends of the following example:

Example 159
"[T]he employer can summarily dismiss the employee for any reason or no reason . . . ." Pine River, 333 N.W.2d at 627.

Also use four periods when you omit language from the beginning of a sentence inside a quotation:

Example 160
"Where the hiring is for an indefinite term, as in this case, the employment is said to be at-will. . . . [T]he employee is under no obligation to remain on the job." Pine River, 333 N.W.2d at 627.

To get the spacing right when you use four periods you must keep in mind which period is the sentence-ending period. If nothing is omitted from the end of a sentence, the sentence-ending period immediately follows the last word in the sentence. That's why there's no space between "at-will" and the period after it in Example 160. If language is omitted from the end of a sentence, the ellipsis follows the last word. That's why there's a space between "reason" and the period that follows it in Example 159; there's always a space before the first period of an ellipsis. The sentence-ending period in Example 159 is the one with no space between it and the final set of quotation marks.

Also use four periods to indicate that you've omitted one or more entire paragraphs from a long quotation. Indent the four periods and put them on a separate line.

If you underline something in your quotation that was not underlined or italicized in the original, put the phrase "emphasis added" or "emphasis supplied" in a parenthetical at the end of your citation:

Example 161
When the employment is at-will, "the employer can summarily dismiss the employee for any reason or no reason." Pine River, 333 N.W.2d at 627 (emphasis added).

Note that the "e" in emphasis added" is not capitalized, and that the period at the end of the citation is placed after the last parenthesis, outside the parenthetical.

If you add something within a quotation, put whatever you add in brackets:

Example 162
"This means that the employer can summarily dismiss the employee for any reason or no reason, and that the [at-will] employee, on the other hand, is under no obligation to remain on the job." <u>Pine River</u>, 333 N.W.2d at 627.

Avoid putting legal terms in quotation marks. Words that are used only in legal contexts, such as *res ipsa loquitur* and *collateral estoppel*, never need to be in quotation marks. But many words have both an everyday meaning and a technical legal meaning. For example, many statutes have a special definition of "person" that includes things such as corporations that aren't normally called "persons." In that situation, you may want to use quotation marks to show you are using the technical legal meaning of an ordinary word:

Example 163
Intercorp was a "person" under section 1961(4).

But quotation marks add clutter to your sentences and make them harder to read. If the meaning is clear without them, leave them out. If it's a close call, put them in the first time you use the word and then drop them:

Example 164
The Eighth Circuit uses a two-pronged test that requires both *"relatedness"* and *"continuity"* to establish a pattern of racketeering. <u>Id.</u> The allegations in the Complaint fail to satisfy the *relatedness* prong as to Intercorp.

11 Authority

Always cite authority for your legal arguments. Legal authority is the foundation of any legal argument. So don't forget to cite authority for every statement you make about the law. And do it immediately—as soon as you make any statement about the law.

In an argument to a court, if you rely on an authority that's hard to find—such as an unpublished case or an obscure regulation—attach a copy to your memo or brief. In an office memo, attach a copy of any authority that's critical to the issue you've analyzed.

Use mandatory authority as your foundation and other authority to fill in gaps. Constitutions, statutes, cases, and rules have the force of law. They are called primary authority. Primary authority in your jurisdiction is called mandatory authority. It controls the outcome of your case. Your discussion or argument of an issue should begin with and focus on mandatory authority. On an issue of state law, that might be statutes in your state or cases decided by the highest court in your state. Use mandatory authority to cover as much of an issue as you can.

Primary authority from other jurisdictions is called persuasive authority. If you have mandatory authority in your favor, don't back it up with persuasive authority. This will only dilute the force of your mandatory authority. For example, don't use a case from outside your jurisdiction to back up a favorable case from your jurisdiction:

Example 165
A repair remedy fails of its essential purpose when the seller fails to make repairs within a reasonable time. <u>Kelynack v. Yamaha USA</u>, 394 N.W.2d 17, 20 (Mich. Ct. App. 1986); <u>Jacobs v. Rosemount</u>, 310 N.W.2d 71, 75 (Minn. 1981).

If the issue is controlled by Michigan law, the second case cited adds nothing because it's from another state. If the point has been decided in your jurisdiction, be secure. Only if the point is uncertain in your jurisdiction should you turn to persuasive authority.

Law review articles, treatises, and encyclopedias may be brilliant commentaries, but they are not law. They are called secondary authority. Only if there is no primary authority on point should you begin with secondary authority. Use secondary authority to explain primary authority and to fill in gaps in the law.

Be aware that some secondary sources carry more weight with courts than others. A law review article by the foremost scholar in the field is far stronger than one written by a student. A quotation from *Prosser and Keeton on Torts* is far stronger than a quotation from *Torts in a Nutshell*.

If you find helpful secondary authority cited or quoted in a case, when you cite that authority you can raise its status by citing it to the case. The citation is strongest if you cite the case and put the secondary authority in a parenthetical:

Example 166
Public duties created by statute cannot be the basis of a negligence action. <u>Calmanson v. Massey</u>, 574 So. 2d 109 (Fla. 1991) (<u>quoting</u> Restatement (Second) Torts sec. 288 (1965)).

Avoid using the words *primary authority*, *mandatory authority*, *persuasive authority*, and *secondary authority* in your memos and briefs. These words are used to teach law students about the proper use of authority but are not generally used by lawyers or courts. For example, you wouldn't see the following sentence in the work of a lawyer or judge:

Example 167
Hill is *mandatory authority* for this case.

Rather, it might be expressed as follows:

Example 168
Hill *controls* this case.

Don't cite a case for a rule that comes directly out of a statute. When a statute is your primary authority, it is the strongest citation you can give. That's why the case citation in the following example is unnecessary:

Example 169
Section 2-302 provides that if a contract was unconscionable at the time it was made, a court may refuse to enforce it. Worldwide Music v. CD City, 578 N.E.2d 80 (N.Y. 1991).

We don't need Worldwide to tell us section 2-302 says what it says. We need cases to tell us things the statute *doesn't* tell us, like the meaning of "unconscionable."

If a federal case applied state law, tell which state's law. If a federal district court is in Texas, it doen't mean the court will always apply Texas law on issues not controlled by federal law. Principles of conflicts of law determine what state's law a federal court will apply. So if you cite a federal case on an issue of state law, always say what state's law the federal court applied:

Example 170
The circumstances under which a contract will be held unconscionable were defined in Chatlos Systems v. National Cash Register Corp., 635 F.2d 1081 (3rd Cir. 1980). There the Third Circuit, *interpreting New Jersey's version of section 2-302*, held that a contract is unconscionable when one party has no meaningful choice but to deal with the other party. Id. at 1085.

Although the federal court in Example 170 applied New Jersey law to the case before it, the case is not a "New Jersey case." Only cases decided by state courts in New Jersey are

New Jersey cases. The decision of a federal court applying New Jersey state law may be strongly persuasive in New Jersey state courts, but it is not binding on them.

Cases—unlike fine wines—don't necessarily improve with age. Although our judicial system is based on the principle of stare decisis, the law is always changing. Sometimes a court overturns an old rule with a single stroke. Other times a court will gradually chip away at an old rule until there's nothing left of it. That's why an old case that hasn't been overruled isn't necessarily a good one. You must Shepardize the case and track it to the present to see how the courts have treated it.

If the case hasn't been cited for many years, you must look at all the surrounding circumstances to determine whether it's still good law. If it's in a stable area of the law, chances are it's still good. But if it's in an area of the law that has changed greatly, you must carefully analyze how the case fits into the changed judicial landscape.

A new rule stated in a new case, on the other hand, is guaranteed to be good for now because the courts haven't had any opportunity to chip away at it. But because the case has not yet stood the test of time, the rule in it may be vulnerable to major revisions in cases shortly following it. It's like a new car: it hasn't suffered from wear and tear, but it may have a major factory defect that won't show up until it's been driven a while.

It is therefore impossible to state categorically that new cases are better than old ones or vice versa. You are in the best position if you can rely on both; the most solid rule is one that comes from an old case and has been recently reaffirmed. When you have such a rule, you can cite both the old case it came from and the most recent case in which it has been reaffirmed:

Example 171
In a fraud action, damages are limited to out-of-pocket losses. Martin v. Stoltz, 430 N.W.2d 207, 213 (Minn. 1990); Lukes v. Hamm, 72 N.W. 812 (Minn. 1897).

If the old case was cited in the new one, you can use a parenthetical phrase for whichever case is less important to your issue. If the new case is more important, cite the old one in parentheses:

Example 172
In a fraud action, damages are limited to out-of-pocket losses. Martin v. Stoltz, 430 N.W.2d 207, 213 (Minn. 1990) (citing Lukes v. Hamm, 72 N.W. 812 (Minn. 1897)).

If the old case is more important, cite the new one in parentheses:

Example 173
In a fraud action, damages are limited to out-of-pocket losses. Lukes v. Hamm, 72 N.W. 812 (Minn. 1897) (cited in Martin v. Stoltz, 430 N.W.2d 207, 213 (Minn. 1990)).

In your discussion or argument, work with whichever case has the most comprehensive analysis of the relevant point of law.

Note the two parentheses spooning at the end of Examples 172 and 173. The first ends the smaller parenthetical with the court and year, the second ends the larger parenthetical.

A case may be helpful even though the result goes against you. Suppose you want to ask a court to set aside a settlement your client agreed to because your client entered into it by mistake. In your research, you find twenty cases in which the court refused such a request and none in which the court granted it. No doubt about it—things look bad.

But it's not over yet. Legal arguments are not evaluated by counting cases. The number of cases going against the party in your client's position does show a tendency of the court. It does not determine the result in your case.

You may be able to argue that something in your case distinguishes it from the others, and that under the rule applied in those cases, the result should be different. You may even find helpful statements in the other cases such as "If the circumstances in this case were X, we might have reached a different result." If you have X circumstances in your case, you're in great shape.

So don't be quick to give up when the *results* of the cases you find are not favorable. Read those cases carefully. Look for a favorable rule, distinguishable facts, explicit statements about what might have led to a different result. When the case law gives you lemons, make lemonade.

Parenthetical phrases are for the facts of unimportant cases. Don't put the facts of an important case in parentheses. Parentheses signal the reader that what's inside them is incidental.

Parenthetical phrases work best when you have a series of cases serving as additional support on a point for which you have other, more important, authority:

Example 174
Courts in other jurisdictions have held that a delay in making repairs of a month or less can cause a limited remedy to fail of its essential purpose: Albeniz v. Southtown Tractor, 516 A.2d 823 (N.H. 1986) (remedy failed where tractor not repaired for three weeks); Shorter v. Allied Indus., 426 N.W.2d 877 (Minn. 1988) (remedy failed where drill press not repaired for one month); Systems Design v. AAA Boiler, Inc., 737 P.2d 619 (Ore. 1987) (remedy failed where boiler not repaired for one month).

Because parentheses interrupt the flow of a sentence, they should also be used sparingly in your text. Don't throw loose thoughts into parentheses, like someone rebuilding a car engine who discovers leftover parts and throws them in the back seat. If something belongs in a sentence, take the time to put it in its rightful place.

Don't cite or quote headnotes. Headnotes are one-paragraph summaries at the beginnings of cases. They are supplied by the publisher as a convenience to the reader. Because they are not written by the court, they are not part of the opinion. Use them as a research tool; don't rely on them as authority.

Cite as many cases as you need and no more. The question most commonly asked by students working on a memo or brief is "How many cases should I cite?" The answer is "As many as you need." You must cite some authority for your legal argument, but if one controlling case covers all the points you need to make, then that's the only case you need.

There is a limit to the number of cases you can effectively include in a memo or brief, especially if you must write within a page limit. Generally, it's better to deal with a few cases thoroughly than many superficially. Quality is more important than quantity. String citations are rarely necessary or effective, and when you are discussing a settled principle they are redundant. Use them only when you're dealing with a principle of law that is unsettled in your jurisdiction and the quantity of favorable authority outside your jurisdiction is critical.

It's hard to tell whether you've found all the relevant authority. The second most commonly asked question by students working on a memo or brief is: "How do I know when I've done enough research?" Hard question. Often you can tell you've found everything because you reach a closed loop where all the cases refer to one another. Other times you know you're finished because you simply run out of time. If neither of these things happens, it's reasonable to quit after you've carefully and thoroughly used the research techniques you learned in your legal research course and found authority that seems to cover your issue.

As you gain experience, you'll develop a better feel for when you've done enough. But there's so much law these days—with the amount growing exponentially—even experienced lawyers are plagued by insecurity about whether they've found everything. Unfortunately, sometimes you don't find out about the authority you missed until you get your opponent's brief. Other times, if you're lucky, the court will help you in its opinion by citing favorable authority you missed. Just do the best you can, and try to leave at least twenty-five percent of your time for writing.

Treat "factors" and "requirements" differently. Statutes and common law rules are often divided into parts. These parts are called variously *factors, requirements, elements, tests, criteria,* etc. You must consistently call them whatever the statute or case calls them, even if it's—what were they thinking?—*prongs*.

You must also pay close attention to the meaning of these different words. There is a critical difference between a *factor* and a *requirement* or *element*. A *factor* must be considered, but a party may do poorly under it and still win if the party does well under other *factors*. A *requirement* or *element*, on the other hand, must be met or the party loses, regardless of how well the party meets other *requirements* or *elements*.

Parties *meet* (or *satisfy*) or *fail* requirements and elements. But talking about *meeting* or *failing* a factor can be confusing, especially when the factor is stated in "whether" form. Suppose courts decide whether to set aside an agreement for mistake using a four-factor test. The first factor considers "whether there were extensive negotiations." If your client wants to get out of a settlement agreement and didn't have extensive negotiations, did that client *meet* or *fail* this factor? From the standpoint of getting out of the agreement, it seems like your client *met* the factor. But looking at the language of the factor alone, it seems like your client *failed* it. Avoid this ambiguity by saying something like: "Under the first factor, the lack of extensive negotiations weighs in favor of setting aside the agreement" or "The agreement should be set aside under the first factor because the negotiations were not extensive."

Parts called by other names—such as *tests, criteria,* and *prongs*—may be treated like either *factors* or *requirements,* depending on the context. Make sure you know how the parts of the statute or rule you're applying are treated, and construct your analysis or argument accordingly.

12 Office Memoranda

The chapters so far have covered legal writing piece by piece, a word or phrase at a time. This chapter explains how to put all the pieces together in an *office memorandum*—called an *office memo* for short. When you get your first law job, an office memo will probably be your first assignment. Your boss will ask you for a memo answering a particular legal question related to a client's situation. This chapter explains how to write one.

Do a first draft early. The advice in this chapter on the structure of a legal analysis is based on the assumption that you've taken care of the content by adequately researching and analyzing the issues. But don't wait to start writing until you feel your analysis is perfect. The act of writing is often an important step in clarifying your thinking. While the analysis is swirling around in your head, it's hard to see gaps in logic and flaws in organization. When you make the analysis stand still on paper, the defects become apparent.

So do a first draft early, even if it's sloppy. Then you'll have time to rethink an issue or run back to the library before the deadline hits. You'll also have time to put the draft aside for a day or two and then give it a fresh look. Time away from a draft is essential for good editing. It gives you the perspective you often lose in the heat of writing. It also gives your subconscious a chance to work on the draft. If you're like me, you'll wake up in the middle of the night to the realization that you missed an issue or skipped a step in the analysis. Keep a pad and pen on the nightstand. If someone sleeps next to you, learn to write in the dark.

Be objective in an office memo. Although your answer in an office memo to the question you've been asked should be objective, that doesn't mean you can't take a stand. Objectivity refers to the process by which you reach your conclusion. You can reach a conclusion that your client will win or lose, as long as you reach it by analyzing the facts and the law from the standpoint of a neutral observer. Anticipate how a judge or jury would see the case and try to predict the result.

You shouldn't have any trouble being objective if the law firm is deciding whether to take a case on a contingent fee. In a contingent-fee case, the firm gets paid only if the client wins. If the case turns out to be a loser, the firm will have lost thousands of dollars in attorneys' time. To protect the firm—and your position within it—you will naturally be conservative in assessing the client's chances of success. The only other time your writing is likely to be as purely objective is in an answer to a law school exam question containing a set of facts followed by the instruction: "Discuss."

Sometimes, however, the economics of the private practice of law can subtly undermine your objectivity and test your scruples. Assume your firm is deciding whether to take a case at an hourly rate. In an hourly-rate case, if the client loses, the firm usually still gets paid. This creates a temptation for you to exaggerate the client's chances of success, because if you make a mistake the consequences for the firm—and for you—will not be so bad. Ethically, however, you should write your memo as objectively as if the case were a contingent-fee case. Even if the prospective client is ready to pay a $50,000 retainer, if he wants to sue the state for instituting daylight saving time because that extra hour of daylight is making his lawn turn brown, you should recommend that the firm refuse the case.

After the firm has accepted a case, the situation becomes slightly different. Now you have a point of view, the point of view of your client, whom you must represent zealously. You will naturally identify with your client, whether it's a flesh-and-blood client in the real world or an imaginary client in a law school assignment. This should inspire you to be thorough and creative, searching out every possible argument in your client's favor.

But don't let your natural identification with your client affect your objectivity. Don't let your desire to win cloud your judgment. Force yourself to be equally thorough and creative in anticipating the other side's arguments. If you don't, you will be giving your boss and the client poor advice, advice that is unrealistically favorable. They need a true picture of the situation to make an informed decision. Tell it like it is.

The format of an office memo varies. Unlike the format of a brief, the format of an office memo is not dictated by any rule or statute. In law school, the recommended format usually includes a Question Presented, a Statement of Facts, a Discussion, and a Conclusion. Sometimes it includes a Brief Answer after the Question Presented. Other times it omits the Brief Answer, but places the Conclusion after the Question Presented instead of at the end. In school, follow the format used in your legal writing text or course.

In law practice, you generally can use any reasonable format, so long as it gets the job done. Often you won't need a Statement of Facts, because your boss will already know the facts and won't want to pay you to write them down. When you do include a Facts section, it should focus narrowly on the facts relevant to the issue you're analyzing.

When I worked for a solo practitioner, I used a format that had two sections: a Summary and a Discussion. The Summary served the functions normally served by the Question Presented, Brief Answer, and Conclusion. By using only a single section, I gained flexibility and saved time. The Summary was probably the only thing my boss ever read.

When you get your first memo assignment, you can ask your supervising attorney whether there is a preferred format. Or you can ask to see some sample memos from the office to get an idea of what's expected. But unless the office requires a certain format without exception, on each assignment you should consider the factors of time, cost, and readability, and adapt your memo accordingly. Ask for a rough estimate of how much time you should spend on the memo, so you won't go over the client's budget. And be sure your boss actually wants a memo; to save time and money, the boss may only want you to report back orally.

Include a thesis paragraph unless it would be redundant or clumsy. The first paragraph in your Discussion generally should introduce and summarize the analysis that follows. When it does, it's called a *thesis paragraph*. It is to the Discussion what a topic sentence is to a paragraph. If possible, it should contain your main conclusion, the governing rule, and the decisive facts.

To illustrate this point and others, I'll work with the following facts:

Carol Sobel owns Sobel's Nursery in upstate New York, where she grows fruit trees. Since 1980, she has been selling trees wholesale to New York retailers. In 1985, she entered into a contract to sell trees to Greenway, Inc., a retailer five times the size of Sobel's Nursery. Greenway insisted on using its form contract, which it refused to allow Sobel to change. A termination clause directly above the place where Sobel signed the contract stated "Buyer or Seller may terminate this contract for any reason upon 30 days' written notice."

Greenway bought trees from Sobel for almost seven years without a problem. Then on March 1, 1992, it surprised Sobel with a written notice stating that it was terminating the contract in 30 days. The notice came at the worst time of year for Sobel; April is her biggest month because most people plant trees in the spring.

Sobel now wants to know if she can recover damages from Greenway. She consulted a lawyer, who asked an associate in the firm to draft a memo on whether the termination clause was unconscionable under New York's version of the Uniform Commercial Code.

Here's a sample thesis paragraph for Sobel's problem:

Example 175
    Sobel is unlikely to recover damages under a theory that the termination clause was unconscionable. Such a clause will be held unconscionable under N.Y. U.C.C. section 2-302 (McKinney 1964) when a seller can show (1) there was no meaningful choice but to deal with the buyer and accept the contract as offered and (2) the clause was unreasonably favorable to the buyer. Worldwide Music v. CD City, 578 N.E.2d 80, 88 (N.Y. 1991). Because Sobel was not forced to deal with Greenway and because the clause gave both parties the same right to terminate the contract, the termination clause is likely to be upheld.

You don't always need a thesis paragraph. It may be redundant when a Brief Answer or Conclusion summarizes the contents of a memo at its start. At least maintain proportion; don't write a thesis paragraph that's almost as long as the analysis it introduces.

A thesis paragraph may also be clumsy when there's no easy way to summarize the analysis. The Discussion may cover several issues, involve several rules, or turn on complex facts. If you try to summarize too much material in a thesis paragraph, it will become indigestable. If you clog a thesis paragraph with citations, it will become unpalatable. The thesis paragraph should whet the reader's appetite, not send the reader searching for Pepto-Bismol.

To let some light into the thesis paragraph, you could expand it to two paragraphs or even more, but this may delay the start of your analysis too long. A better idea is to break it into smaller paragraphs, and place one at the start of each issue.

Discuss issues one at a time in logical order. If you have two or more issues or sub-issues, discuss them separately. Complete one before moving to the next.

Sometimes the issues will be neatly divided for you, such as when a crime or cause of action has several elements. Other times the law will be a mess, and you will have to do the work of separating the issues yourself. When you've separated them, make an outline and move them around until the order makes sense.

Search for an organizing principle. The best one is usually the following: Start with the most important issue and work down to the least important. Always keep in mind that your audience has come for the main attraction and will grow impatient sitting through too many warm-up acts. Try to find an order that gets you quickly to the heart of the analysis.

However, sometimes the most important issue will not be understandable if placed first. And sometimes you'll have issues of equal importance. In these and other situations, you'll need another organizing principle. Here are some likely candidates:

- Procedural before substantive issues
- Liability before damages issues
- Theory that offers complete relief before theory that offers only partial relief
- Statutory causes of action before common law causes of action
- Argument that conduct doesn't fall within a statute before argument that the statute is invalid
- Theory most likely to lead to success to theory least likely
- Simple to complex
- Chronological order
- Order used by the courts in relevant decided cases

The possibilities are endless. Customize the order of your issues to fit the situation.

Organize the discussion of each issue with CRAC. CRAC (pronounced "**see**-rack" to avoid any unwanted connotations) is a tool to help you organize the discussion of a legal issue. It's a slight variation of the better-known IRAC (pronounced "I-rack"). IRAC stands for "Issue," "Rule of law," "Application of rule to facts," and "Conclusion." It's designed to remind you to cover those four elements in that order.

The only difference between CRAC and IRAC is that CRAC starts with a conclusion instead of an issue. Knowing the conclusion at the start helps the reader understand the analysis, just as knowing who did it in a mystery novel makes it easier to spot the clues.

Here's a simple issue discussed in CRAC form:

Example 176
Sobel's contract with Greenway is governed by Article 2 of New York's Uniform Commercial Code. Article 2 governs all transactions in "goods," which are defined in section 2-107 to include "growing crops or other things attached to realty capable of severance without material harm." Sobel grows her trees in the ground, but when she sells them she digs them up and transfers them. Because the trees are severed from the realty without harm, they are goods covered by Article 2.

In Example 176, the first sentence is the conclusion, the second the rule, the third the application, and the fourth the conclusion again. For another example, look at the thesis paragraph in Example 175. CRAC often works well as the structure of a thesis paragraph.

An entire CRAC happens to fit in a single paragraph in Example 176, but usually it won't. The conclusions will stay short, but the rule and application will often be much longer. Sometimes you'll need several paragraphs to fully explain a rule or apply the rule to your facts. You'll see examples with a longer rule and application later in this chapter.

Note that although the first and last sentences of Example 176 are both conclusions in a single CRAC, they are stated differently. This is mainly for reasons of style; starting and ending a short CRAC with identical conclusions would sound mechanical. This is also partly for reasons of function; the first conclusion introduces the analysis and the second concludes it. Your second conclusion can usually be more specific than your first because the reader knows more by the end.

The application element is the most confusingly named. In the application, you bring in the facts of your case that are relevant to deciding the issue, and *apply* the rule to those facts. To the extent necessary, you will *analyze* those facts in light of the relevant rule of law.   Think of the "A" in CRAC as also standing for "Analysis" so you'll remember to analyze your facts in your "A" section when necessary.

Often you will have an overriding CRAC on a main issue encompassing smaller CRACs on sub-issues. For example, when the main issue is whether there was a battery, the sub-issues are the elements of a battery: (1) intentionally causing a (2) harmful or offensive contact with (3) the person of another. The CRAC pattern looks like this:

CONCLUSION (on whether there was a battery)
RULE (battery has three elements)
APPLICATION
   First Element: Intent
    Conclusion
    Rule
    Application
    Conclusion
   Second Element: Harmful or offensive contact
    Conclusion
    Rule
    Application
    Conclusion
   Third Element: Person of another
    Conclusion
    Rule
    Application
    Conclusion
CONCLUSION (on whether there was a battery)

The three smaller CRACs in Example 176 make up the "A" of the larger CRAC.

When a legal discussion becomes complex, with intertwining and overlapping legal issues, it may become impossible to stick with CRAC. That's okay. Let go of CRAC in those situations, and follow the logic of the particular problem you're dealing with. CRAC is a flexible tool to aid you in constructing a legal discussion, not an ironclad mold you must squeeze every issue into.

Explain the rule of law before applying it to your facts.
Usually you will need to explain the relevant legal rule before you can apply it to the facts of your case. In the following example, the rule of law comes from a statute that is not explained enough before it is applied:

Example 177
Sobel is unlikely to prevail on a theory of unconscionability. If a contract or any part of it was unconscionable at the time it was made, a court may refuse to enforce it under section 2-302. Sobel did not have to enter into the contract with Greenway because she had other potential customers for her trees. And the clause itself gave both parties an equal right to terminate the contract. Therefore, it is unlikely that the clause was unconscionable under section 2-302.

Because the application of section 2-302 to Sobel's facts in Example 177 comes before the reader has any clear idea of what unconscionability means, the conclusion is unconvincing. You must show every step of your analysis. It's like a high school math test; you don't get credit for the right answer if you don't show your work.

One way to explain a rule is to bring in case law interpreting it. In the following example, after the case's interpretation of the rule is given, that interpretation is applied to Sobel's facts:

Example 178
Sobel is unlikely to prevail on a theory of unconscionability. A court may refuse to enforce a contract or any part of it that was unconscionable at the time it was made under section 2-302. Unconscionability, however, is not defined in section 2-302.

Section 2-302 was interpreted recently by the New York Court of Appeals as it applied to a termination clause in <u>Worldwide Music v. CD City</u>, 578 N.E.2d 80 (N.Y. 1991). The court held that to prevail on a theory that such a clause was unconscionable, a seller must show (1) there was no meaningful choice but to deal with the buyer and accept the contract as offered and (2) the clause was unreasonably favorable to the buyer. <u>Id.</u> at 88.

Although Sobel had to accept the contract as offered, she still had the meaningful choice of refusing to deal with Greenway. When she entered into the contract, she had other potential customers for her trees. The clause also was not unreasonably favorable to Greenway; Sobel had an equal right to terminate the contract at any time. Therefore, it is unlikely that the clause was unconscionable.

Give enough facts about each case you cite to make it meaningful and useful. Example 178 is better than Example 177, but it's still not complete because the writer didn't give any of the facts of <u>Worldwide</u>. Those facts are needed for two purposes. First, they are needed to give meaning to the holding of the case. Second, they are needed so the writer can use them to compare the case to Sobel's case. Only by comparing the facts of the two cases can we decide whether the result in Sobel's case should be the same as the result in <u>Worldwide</u>:

Example 179

Section 2-302 was interpreted recently by the New York Court of Appeals as it applied to a termination clause in <u>Worldwide Music v. CD City</u>, 578 N.E.2d 80 (N.Y. 1991). The clause in <u>Worldwide</u> was contained in a contract negotiated between two large corporations: a wholesale seller of compact discs and a buyer of equal size. It stated that either party had the power to terminate the contract upon 90 days' notice. When the buyer terminated the contract, the seller sued. <u>Id.</u> at 83.

The court held that to prevail on a theory that such a clause was unconscionable, a seller must show (1) there was no meaningful choice but to deal with the buyer and accept the contract as offered and (2) the clause was unreasonably favorable to the buyer. Id. at 88. The seller in Worldwide met neither of these requirements. First, the seller had a meaningful choice not to deal with the buyer because it had other customers it could have sold to and the buyer did not have grossly superior bargaining power. Second, the contract was not unreasonably favorable to the buyer because the seller also had the right to terminate if it received a more favorable offer from one of the buyer's competitors. The court therefore held that the clause was not unconscionable. Id.

Sobel meets neither of the requirements set forth in Worldwide. Although Sobel had to accept the contract as offered, she still had the meaningful choice of refusing to deal with Greenway. When she entered into the contract she had other potential customers for her trees. The clause also was not unreasonably favorable to Greenway; like the seller in Worldwide, Sobel had an equal right to terminate the contract at any time. Therefore, it is unlikely that the clause was unconscionable.

The structure of the analysis in Example 179 is a modified CRAC because Worldwide splits the issue of unconscionability into two sub-issues: "no meaningful choice" and "unreasonably favorable." These two rules appear in the second paragraph, followed by an application of both in the third paragraph. The structure is therefore CRRAAC. If the application had been more extensive, a separate CRAC for each sub-issue would have been necessary. That's what will happen in the next section when counterarguments are added.

The description of Worldwide in Example 179 follows a pattern you can use as a model for other case descriptions. First introduce the case with a statement about some aspect of it that creates a smooth transition. Then give a full citation. Then give the facts of the case. Finally, give the rule and the holding.

Sometimes a case has separate facts that relate to separate issues. If you use the case in your analysis of more than one issue, you may not need to give all the facts the first time you mention the case. You can split them between the issues if the separate facts relating to each issue are understandable on their own.

Sometimes you will only need to give a few facts about a case to make it meaningful and useful, and sometimes you won't need to give any. You may not need to give any facts about a case when you cite it for a rule of law that is well established, is stated in general terms, and is not dependent on the facts of the case from which it came. This is often true of procedural rules, such as "Summary judgment is a drastic remedy" or "An appellate court will not hear arguments on appeal that were not raised in the trial court."

On the other hand, you may need to give a complete version of the facts of a case. They may be necessary to clarify the reason for the court's holding, to show that the holding is not what it appears to be, or to make a subtle distinction between the cited case and yours. The more debatable your interpretation of the case, the more facts you need to give.

Remember the rule is to give *enough* facts. What is enough changes with each case you use and with each context you use it in.

First give the analysis supporting your conclusion on an issue—even if it's against your client—then discuss counterarguments. In the sample office memos in the legal writing texts I've seen, the conclusion has always been in favor of the writer's client. The discussion of Sobel's case in Example 179 illustrates that a conclusion can also go against the writer's client.

The discussion of Sobel's case in Example 179 also helps illustrate the rule that you should give the analysis that supports your conclusion first. The writer has concluded that Sobel cannot show unconscionability and has given the analysis supporting that conclusion. If the writer had concluded that Sobel could show unconscionability, then the support for that conclusion would have come first.

After the analysis supporting your conclusion on an issue, go on to discuss any counterarguments. Gathering your counterarguments at the end of each issue prevents your analysis from resembling a ping-pong match and giving the reader a sore neck. Using this strategy, the final paragraph in Example 179 might be expanded as follows:

Example 180

Sobel meets neither of the requirements set forth in Worldwide. Under the first requirment, Sobel had the meaningful choice of refusing to deal with Greenway. Like the seller in Worldwide, when she entered into the contract she had other potential customers.

The differences between our case and Worldwide are not significant enough to warrant a different conclusion here under the first requirement. Greenway was five times the size of Sobel's Nursery, while the parties in Worldwide were of equal size. And the contract in our case was a form contract which Greenway refused to negotiate, while the contract in Worldwide was negotiated by the parties. But it is unlikely that these differences establish that Sobel had no meaningful choice because Greenway did not have the "grossly superior bargaining power" required by Worldwide under the first requirement.

Under the second requirement, the clause was probably not unreasonably favorable to Greenway. The clauses in Worldwide and Sobel's case are almost identical. Like the seller in Worldwide, Sobel had an equal right to terminate the contract at any time.

The only difference between the clauses is the length of the notice period: 90 days in Worldwide as opposed to 30 here. If Greenway can more easily find other sources for trees on short notice than Sobel can find other buyers, Sobel might be able to argue that the shortness of the notice period was unreasonably favorable to Greenway. This fact needs to be investigated.

Finally, whether Greenway exercised its right to terminate at a time that was unreasonably favorable to it is irrelevant; section 2-302 measures unconscionability at the time the contract was made. Sobel therefore probably cannot meet Worldwide's second requirement.

Because of the similarity between Sobel's case and Worldwide, Sobel is unlikely to prevail on a theory of unconscionability.

In Example 180, each sub-issue gets its own CRAC. The rules in these CRACs (the first and second requirements from <u>Worldwide</u>) are not repeated in full because they've just been stated in the paragraph on <u>Worldwide</u>.

Tell whether your issue will be decided by a judge or a jury. Issues of law are decided at trial by the trial judge, often referred to impersonally as "the court." Issues of fact are decided by the jury when there is one. Because juries are usually more sympathetic to emotional arguments than judges, your boss will want to know who's going to decide your issue.

Knowing whether an issue is one of fact or law also helps the reader assess the effect of cited cases on your case. When an appellate court holds that a jury's finding of fact was not unreasonable, it's only saying there was enough evidence for the jury to reach that finding. It isn't necessarily agreeing with that finding or saying that in a similar case a jury must reach the same result. So even if you have the same facts in your case, you cannot predict the result with certainty. Temper your conclusions to reflect this uncertainty when you analyze an issue of fact: "The jury will *probably* find . . . ."

When your issue is one of law, you can draw conclusions from case comparisons with more certainty; you have something solid to compare your facts to. An appellate decision that a particular set of facts requires a certain result as a matter of law requires a court faced with similar facts to reach the same result.

Case law and statutes determine whether an issue is one of fact or law. Find out what kind of issue yours is and include that information in your analysis:

Example 181
Although unconscionability is not defined in section 2-302, *subsection (1) provides that the issue of unconscionability is an issue of law for the court.*

Once you've told who will decide your issue, you can insert reminders into your conclusions:

Example 182
Therefore, *a court is not likely to hold that* the termination clause was unconscionable.

Remember: judges *hold* or *rule* on issues of law; juries and judges *find* on issues of fact.

Lawyers and judges use phrases such as *jury issue* and *jury question* to talk about issues of fact even though issues of fact are decided by a trial judge when there is no jury. That's why your conclusion on an issue of fact can properly say "*The jury will probably find*," even though there might not be a jury if the case goes to trial.

Track the language of cases and statutes when you apply them to your facts. Tracking is just a variation of parallelism, which is covered in chapter 3 on style. The idea is to match the language you use about your case to the language used in a cited case or statute. For example, since <u>Worldwide</u> talks about "meaningful choice," when you apply that rule to Sobel's facts you should say "Sobel had a *meaningful choice*," not "Sobel had other *viable options*." Tracking makes your writing easier to follow. And if you're trying to show that your case is controlled by a cited case or statute, it makes your writing more persuasive too.

Use transitions that point both ways. Transitions are the glue that holds your discussion or argument together. They come in all sizes. They can be one word, such as "however" or "furthermore," or they can be a full sentence or more. Whatever size a transition is, ideally it should point both ways: it should tell the reader where you've been and where you're going, and by doing so tell the reader where you are in the structure of your discussion or argument.

For example, suppose you've just taken a paragraph to describe <u>Worldwide</u>, a case in which the court held a termination clause was not unconscionable. Now you want to begin describing another case in which the court held a different termination clause was not unconscionable. Don't start the second paragraph without a transition, like this:

Example 183
In <u>Gianni Sportswear v. T.J. Maxx, Inc.</u>, 572 N.E.2d 32 (N.Y. 1989) a clothing manufacturer sued a clothing retailer when the retailer terminated its contract.

This sentence gives no clue where the paragraph is going or how it relates to what came before. A string of paragraphs beginning with "In [case name]" is a common giveaway that what should be a well-organized analysis is merely an undigested mass of case law.

The following sentence would have provided a better transition:

Example 184
The court also held a termination clause was not unconscionable in <u>Gianni Sportswear v. T.J. Maxx, Inc.</u>, 572 N.E.2d 32 (N.Y. 1989).

This transition lets the reader know where the paragraph is going by immediately telling what the court held in <u>Gianni Sportswear</u>. It also reminds the reader of what came before by simply including the word "also," which says "I've just finished talking about a case where a termination clause was held not to be unconscionable, and now I'm going to talk about another one."

But the transition could be even better:

Example 185
The court also held a termination clause was not unconscionable even though it provided for only 45 days' notice in <u>Gianni Sportswear v. T.J. Maxx, Inc.</u>, 572 N.E.2d 32 (N.Y. 1989).

This transition gives the reader plenty of information about what's coming and how it relates to what came before. Try to make all your transitions do that.

Use subheadings generously even though they aren't required.
In an office memo, only main headings (like **DISCUSSION**) are
required. But you should use subheadings whenever they'd be
helpful. In any long Discussion they are a virtual necessity.
They may even be helpful in a long Statement of Facts. Look
for ways to break up anything longer than five pages.

Subheadings in an office memo don't have to be complete
sentences like the point headings in a brief. Since you're not
trying to persuade, they can be single words, like "Offer,"
"Acceptance," and "Consideration." But avoid subheadings that
convey no information, such as "Part 1."

Logic requires that you have at least two subheadings on
each level of organization. If you have an "A," you must at
least have a "B"; if you have a "1," you must at least have a "2."

If your memo is long and you've used subheadings, include
a table of contents. It isn't required either, but your reader will
appreciate it.

Don't put new material in your Conclusion. Most office memos
have a section at the end titled "Conclusion." Here you should
put your final conclusion on the main issue you've discussed, as
well as any conclusions on important sub-issues. Your final
conclusion and the grounds for it shouldn't surprise the reader.
The conclusions in your CRACs should have made your position
clear. In the Conclusion section, you simply collect all those
conclusions in one place for the reader's convenience.

In your Conclusion you should also summarize the reasoning
that led to your conclusions. This amounts to a brief summary
of your Discussion and should generally be about a paragraph
long. Don't include citations; the reader can find them in your
Discussion.

The Conclusion is no place for new material. Don't raise an
interesting policy argument or mention a case for the first time
in your Conclusion. Other than your final conclusion, the only
new material that should go in the Conclusion is your recommendation about what to do next.

Express your conclusions as precisely as possible. Your boss must make a decision based on your memo. A yes or no answer in your Conclusion will make that decision easy. But the facts and the law rarely lead to such definite answers. Take a stand if you can, but don't give a definite answer when the answer is less certain. The points you earn for decisiveness when your boss reads the memo will be lost when your boss loses the case.

Some imprecision is justified because law isn't an exact science. Assigning a specific percentage to Sobel's chances, as in "Sobel has a 75% chance of success," creates an illusion of exactitude where there is none. And you should never give an answer that could be interpreted by the client as a guarantee.

But even though your answer is uncertain and somewhat imprecise, it shouldn't be completely vague. Describe the degree of your uncertainty as precisely as possible: "A court is *unlikely* to hold that the termination clause is unconscionable," "The federal court *almost certainly* has jurisdiction over Chen's claim," "Sportco will *probably* succeed in establishing that Efron was acting within the scope of her employment." One way to increase the precision of your answer is to pinpoint the source of any uncertainty: "A jury will probably find that Dr. Anton was negligent *if we can persuade the court to apply a national standard of care.*"

Avoid conclusions that are completely vague, such as "Sobel *has a chance* of winning" or "Sobel *may* win." Sentences formed with "possibly" are similarly vague. And "Sobel *should* win" can be ambiguous; it could mean "Sobel will win" or "A victory for Sobel would be a just result."

Finally, don't overhedge in a conclusion, as in this example:

Example 186
It *appears* Sobel *may* have a good *chance* of winning in a suit against Greenway.

"Appears" and "may" dilute Sobel's "chance" so much that they make the reader wonder whether it really is "good." This makes the conclusion almost meaningless. If you find yourself hedging too much in a conclusion, try writing it while listening to the theme song from *Rocky*.

13 Questions Presented

Briefs and office memos start with a question under the heading Question Presented or Issue. A good Question helps the reader grasp the subject of the brief or memo quickly. And the process of formulating Questions will help you identify and clarify issues. This in turn will help you focus your writing in the discussion or argument that follows. This chapter explains how to construct a Question step by step.

Choose clarity over completeness. Tradition requires that each Question be squeezed into a single sentence. But complex issues aren't always comfortable in cramped quarters. Coaxing them in takes time and hard work. Frustration can tempt you to abandon the principles of plain English.

Don't do it. If forced to choose, sacrifice completeness for clarity. You can always put missing details in your discussion or argument. A logically complete Question is useless if it's so long and convoluted no one can follow it. A Question should be easy to understand in a single reading; it shouldn't be something the reader has to study.

Avoid starting Questions with "Whether." No matter how many lawyers still do it, starting a Question with whether is bad grammar. Don't say: "Whether lost profits can be recovered in a fraud action"; say "Can lost profits be recovered in a fraud action?" Complete sentences make stronger Questions.

Start with the law and end with the facts. Questions should generally include both law (a reference to a legal rule) and facts. To create a context in which the reader can understand and evaluate the facts, it's generally best to put the law at the beginning of the Question. The law in the following Question is the common law duty to rescue:

Example 187
Does a store owner have *a duty to rescue* an injured person in the store when the person is not a customer and was injured outside the store?

If the law comes from a statute, identify the statute. If the statute is known by name, use the name in your Question and save the citation for your discussion or argument:

Example 188
Does a buyer have a claim under Minnesota's Lemon Law when the buyer's car was out of service for three months during the warranty period but was working perfectly by the time of trial?

If the rule of law comes from case law, you generally don't need to identify its source. That's why there's no reference to the source of the common-law rule in the Question in Example 187. However, when a single case dominates an issue, you may want to include its short-form name in the Question:

Example 189
Is there personal jurisdiction over Sportco in California under International Shoe when Sportco has no retail stores in the state but makes an average of five sales a year to California customers by mail order?

Even if you do mention a case in a Question, don't clutter the Question with a citation.

In each Question above, the "when" is a rough dividing line between the law and the facts. If you're having trouble writing a Question, try the formula "[law] when [facts]?" Or you can try something like "[law] even though [facts]?"

A Question without facts does little to inform the reader of an office memo and nothing to persuade the reader of a brief:

Example 190
Was the termination clause unconscionable under section
2-302 of the Uniform Commercial Code?

Only if the format allowed you to precede a Question like
Example 190 with a short paragraph of facts would it be
effective. But that format isn't used in many law schools or
courts. You're probably going to have to pick the top two or
three determinative facts for your Question and leave it to your
discussion or argument to supply the rest.

The facts you include in your Question should be specific.
Don't editorialize, as in the following example:

Example 191
Was a termination clause unconscionable under section 2-302
of the Uniform Commercial Code when it was used by a buyer
to victimize a smaller seller?

This vague characterization of the facts neither informs nor
persuades. Example 196 makes the point made in Example 191
with specific facts and without editorializing.

Decide whether to use roles or names to refer to the parties.
Using real-life roles such as "buyer" and "seller" often works
well in a Question in a brief, because an appellate court is
unfamiliar with the parties. Also, an appellate court is
concerned not just with the particular parties in the case before
it, but with how its resolution of the issue will affect the law and
the conduct of citizens in its jurisdiction.

A lawyer requesting an office memo, however, doesn't have
these broad concerns but rather the specific concerns of an
advocate for a particular client. Using the names of the parties
may therefore be appropriate in an office memo:

Example 192
Does Mushki have a fraud claim against Import Auto for failing
to tell him that the used car he bought had transmission
problems even though no one at Import Auto made any
representations about the condition of the transmission?

You may also want to use names in a brief if for some strategic reason you want to focus the court's attention on the particular parties.

Litigation roles (such as *Plaintiff* or *Appellant*) are usually ineffective in a Question because they give no information about the parties. Don't use them unless you're dealing with a procedural issue or talking about the defendant in a criminal case.

However you refer to the parties, if you have more than one Question, be consistent. Don't refer to "buyer" and "seller" in one Question and "Greenway" and "Sobel's Nursery" in another.

Don't include legal conclusions in Questions. Remember, a Question defines an issue by giving the controlling law and facts. It should not contain its own answer in the form of a legal conclusion. It should be left open so it can be answered by the discussion or argument that follows it.

The following examples from a defamation case illustrate this principle. Suppose the main issue is whether a person who made defamatory statements is protected by a privilege. A privilege will exist if the person made the statements on a proper occasion, with a proper motive, and with reasonable grounds. The main issue thus has three sub-issues. The following Question is a fake because it contains legal conclusions that prematurely answer the Question:

Example 193
Were Arkin's defamatory statements about Dr. Hall privileged when he made them on a proper occasion, with a proper motive, and with reasonable grounds?

Because each sub-issue is presented in the form of a legal conclusion, the Question can have only one answer: yes. Substituting specific facts for the legal conclusions keeps the Question open:

Example 194
Were Arkin's defamatory statements about Dr. Hall privileged when he made them while giving an unfavorable job reference to prevent Dr. Hall from getting a job because he knew a patient had died after being operated on by Dr. Hall?

State only main issues in Questions. Questions are like headings. They should be in proportion to the body of the discussion or argument they introduce. Minor issues don't need to be covered in your Questions at all. Important sub-issues can be covered by implication.

For example, suppose you were writing an office memo on the defamation issue that is the subject of Examples 193 and 194. If the three sub-issues take up ten pages each, a separate Question for each would be reasonable. On the other hand, if your whole Discussion was five pages long, having a separate Question for each of the sub-issues would make your memo top-heavy.

Don't try to have it both ways by squeezing the main issue, the three sub-issues, and the facts into one Question:

Example 195
Were Arkin's defamatory statements about Dr. Hall made on a proper occasion, with a proper motive, and with reasonable grounds so as to be privileged when he made them while giving an unfavorable job reference to prevent Dr. Hall from getting a job because he knew a patient had died after being operated on by Dr. Hall?

Instead, state the main issue explicitly and include facts that *imply* the sub-issues. That's the technique used in Example 194. There the three facts imply the three sub-issues.

Carefully select and emphasize undisputed facts to make a Question persuasive. All the Questions above (except Example 191) are objective and thus suitable for an office memo. The facts in each are balanced and they fairly summarize each situation.

In a brief or in a memorandum of law to a trial court, your Questions should be persuasive. To make them persuasive, you must carefully select and emphasize facts that support your argument. If possible, choose undisputed facts; if the court doubts your premises it is unlikely to reach the answer you want.

A persuasive Question for Sobel might emphasize the inequality in bargaining power between her and Greenway:

Example 196
Was a 30-day termination clause unconscionable under section 2-302 of the Uniform Commercial Code when the clause was contained in the buyer's form contract that the buyer refused to negotiate, and the buyer was five times the size of the seller?

A persuasive Question for Greenway might emphasize that the clause was the same for both parties and that Greenway did not coerce Sobel into the contract:

Example 197
Was a clause giving both a buyer and a seller the equal right to terminate their contract on 30 days' notice unconscionable to the seller under section 2-302 of the Uniform Commercial Code when the seller had other potential customers at the time it entered into the contract?

Some lawyers think a persuasive Question should be designed to elicit a yes answer from the court. I think that as long as a Question is clear, it doesn't matter whether it's designed to elicit a yes or a no. However, when you have more than one Question, each Question should be designed to elicit the same answer. Thus, if you have three Questions, the answers should be "yes-yes-yes" or "no-no-no," not "yes-no-yes."

Emphasize your trial court victory in persuasive Questions. In a brief, whichever side won in the trial court should lace its Questions with references to that victory. Although a trial court's rulings on issues of law have little precedential weight, they at least show that a judge who studied the matter agreed with the winner's position. Thus it might help a little for the winner's Questions to begin with: "Did the trial court properly *rule* that . . . ." On the other hand, a trial court's findings on issues of fact carry great weight with an appellate court. The winner is therefore wise to begin Questions relating to issues of fact with "Did the trial court properly *find* that . . . ."

Turn Questions into main point headings in a brief. Point headings serve to divide your brief and summarize your arguments. They must be complete sentences arranged in outline form. Main point headings should correspond to Questions Presented. Turn a Question into a main point heading by changing it into an affirmative statement. Here's Greenway's Question from Example 197 turned into a main point heading:

Example 198
I. THE TERMINATION CLAUSE WAS NOT UNCONSCIONABLE UNDER SECTION 2-302 BECAUSE SOBEL'S NURSERY HAD OTHER POTENTIAL CUSTOMERS AT THE TIME IT ENTERED INTO THE CONTRACT AND THE CLAUSE GAVE BOTH PARTIES AN EQUAL RIGHT TO TERMINATE THE CONTRACT.

If you used the parties' roles in your Questions, you generally should switch to names in your point headings. Greenway switched from "seller" to "Sobel's Nursery" in Example 198. By using roles in the Questions you should have satisfied the court's desire to understand the broader context of the issues of law presented in your case. In the point headings, you can get down to business and focus on the particular parties.

If you have three Questions, you should have three main point headings, and they should be in the same order as the Questions. You can use as many subheadings as you need under the main point headings. Just be careful not to interrupt the flow of an argument by chopping it into tiny pieces. If the main point heading in Example 198 were divided into a main point heading and subheadings, here's how it would look in a Table of Contents:

Example 199

I. THE TERMINATION CLAUSE WAS NOT UNCONSCIONABLE UNDER SECTION 2-302 OF THE UNIFORM COMMERCIAL CODE.

   A. Sobel's Nursery had a meaningful choice not to deal with Greenway because it had other potential customers at the time it entered into the contract.

   B. The clause was not unreasonably favorable to Greenway because it gave both parties an equal right to terminate the contract.

You can see that by adding subheadings in Example 199, Greenway was able to shorten the main point heading, making it easier to read and understand. By adding subheadings, Greenway also was able to add information that couldn't be squeezed into a single main point heading.

By tradition, main headings are written in all capital letters. Subheadings are written like normal sentences. Subheadings are underlined in your Argument but not in your Table of Contents. Make sure that your Table of Contents includes every subheading you use.

As with subheadings in a memo, logic requires at least two subheadings on each level of organization. If you have an "A," you must have a "B"; if you have a "1," you must have a "2." The only exception to this rule occurs when you have only one main point in a brief. That point should be labeled "I" even though there's no "II." Don't ask me why.

14 Argument

A good objective discussion of a legal issue and a good persuasive argument on the same issue have much in common. Both require a mastery of the facts. Both require good research, writing, and analysis. Even their structures are similar. But you need to make several specific changes when you switch from discussion to argument. This chapter explains those changes and the strategy you need to make your writing persuasive.

Borrow from the format of a brief to make a memorandum of law more effective. *Appellate briefs* and *memoranda of law* are the documents lawyers use to argue to courts. A brief is submitted on legal issues to an appellate court. Each jurisdiction has a statute or court rule determining what a brief must contain and in what order. The Statement of Facts and the Argument are always at the heart of a brief. Sections for Questions Presented or Issues, a Table of Contents, a Table of Authorities, and a Conclusion are always included. Sometimes other sections are included, such as Statement of the Case, Opinions Below, Jurisdiction, Statutes Involved, and Summary of the Argument.

One section in a brief that often confuses students is the Conclusion. It has the same name as the Conclusion in an office memo but it serves a different function. In a brief, the Conclusion has traditionally contained nothing except a simple statement of what the party wants the court to do, such as "For the reasons set forth above, Sportco requests that this Court affirm the judgment of the district court." However, some lawyers also use the Conclusion in a brief to summarize their

Argument

127

argument, to make their main point one last time, or to end on a dramatic note. If you want to try this, wait until you get out of law school and make sure the court allows it.

A *memorandum of law* (sometimes called a *trial court brief* or *memorandum of points and authorities*) is submitted on legal issues to a trial court. Unlike an appellate brief, often its format isn't governed by statute or court rule. Different lawyers do them different ways. The sections typically included are an Introduction, a Statement of Facts, an Argument, and a Conclusion.

This simple format works well enough in a short memorandum. But in a long memorandum, you should divide your Argument with point headings and add a Table of Contents. Make it easy for judges to find their way around. A frustrated judge is hard to persuade. Also add any other section from a brief that would make your memorandum clearer and easier to follow.

Tell a compelling story in your Facts. In our system of justice, courts are supposed to decide cases in keeping with existing statutes, administrative rules, and case law. But because reality is infinitely varied and complex, often a dispute won't fall squarely under any particular statute, rule, or case. If it does, it gets settled, and settled early. Disputes that become litigated cases are usually disputes in which it is unclear what law applies or how the law applies.

A court, therefore, usually has some discretion in deciding a case. And because judges are human beings who usually want to do what they believe is right, you should try to influence the exercise of their discretion by showing them that the result you want is not only legally correct but also fair and just. Relying solely on technical legal arguments is poor strategy that ignores human nature.

The best way to get the court on your side early is to tell a compelling story in your Statement of Facts. Writing persuasive facts is a subtle art. You can't just haul out the heaviest adjectives in your vocabulary and dump them on the page. The trick is to write persuasive facts that appear objective. You want the judges to feel that they're simply reading what happened.

The first thing you need to think about is what order to tell the story in. Chronological order is generally the easiest to follow. But since readers tend to identify with whoever is introduced first, you should try to start with your client, even if that means deviating from chronological order. Whatever order you decide on, remember that you don't have to group facts according to who testified to them.

You also need to think about where in the order of events to put background information. If you give it all at the beginning, you won't have to interrupt the action once it starts. But you must not delay the start of the action too long or you'll risk losing the reader. You may have to give much of the background information as you go, inserting details wherever you can without breaking the momentum of the story.

The next two examples show how opposing parties might begin their facts. The case concerns Steven Massey, a fifteen-year-old boy who was chased by a gang of older boys. He sought help from Shirley Rannum at her apartment building. After she ignored him, the gang caught him and severely injured him. Massey sued Rannum for failing to rescue him. Massey's Facts might begin as follows:

Example 200

Fifteen-year-old Steven Massey was walking home alone near downtown Minneapolis a little before midnight on July 8, 1991, when a gang of older boys started chasing him. He tried to elude the gang by running through the yards of the houses on the 700 block of Burns Street. While climbing over a fence, he fell and cut his forehead. But when he heard the gang close behind him, he got up and started running again. The cut bled down his face as he ran. Some blood got into his eyes, making it hard for him to see.

He ran to the apartment building at 700 Burns Street. Out of breath, he ducked into the small lobby and began banging on the inside door and begging to be let in. A few moments later, Shirley Rannum, the owner and caretaker of the building, stuck her head out of her apartment and saw Steven.

The apartment owner's Facts might begin as follows:

Example 201

Shirley Rannum is the owner and caretaker of the apartment building at 700 Burns Street near downtown Minneapolis, and she lives in apartment 101. Because the building is in a rough neighborhood, the inner door of the lobby is always kept locked. Rannum herself was mugged in front of the building in 1989 and had her purse stolen.

On July 8, 1991, Rannum went to bed about 11 p.m. A little before midnight, she was awakened from a deep sleep by someone pounding and shouting in the lobby. She went in her nightgown to the door of her apartment and looked out. Through the inner lobby door, she saw a young man she had never seen before, with blood on his face, demanding to be let in.

Examples 200 and 201 not only start with the client, they also show the facts from the client's point of view. Describe what your client saw, heard, and felt. If your client is a corporation or other entity, find some human beings in it to focus on. Make your client come alive to the court.

Don't embellish facts with emotional adjectives and adverbs. Massey's Facts shouldn't say: "Rannum ignored the pleas for help from the injured, blood-stained youth." The reader already knows that Steven cut his forehead and that the cut bled onto his face. "Rannum shut the door to her apartment, ignoring Steven's pleas for help" is all that's needed to make the point.

So let the facts speak for themselves, but arrange and emphasize them so they also speak for your client. Emphasize favorable facts by placing them at the beginning or end of sentences and paragraphs. De-emphasize unfavorable facts by burying them in the middle of sentences and paragraphs.

Describe favorable facts in vivid detail. Massey's Facts might say: "When Massey's head hit the concrete, his skull was split open." Describe unfavorable facts blandly in general terms. Rannum's Facts might say: "Massey fell, suffering severe head injuries."

Avoid cluttering your Facts. Omit unnecessary dates and times. Omit the source of a fact if isn't important; you don't have to tell who testified to a particular fact as long as you cite the record. Only tell who testified to a fact when you want to for persuasive reasons:

Example 202
Dr. Eva Lehr, head of neurology at the Mayo Clinic, testified that Steven will never regain the full use of his hand.

Finally, don't leave out any important facts, even if they hurt you. There's no hiding anything; you can be sure your opponent will tell the court. By omitting a damaging fact, you lose the chance to present it in a way that minimizes its damage.

If you tell a compelling story, by the end of your Facts the judges will be predisposed to rule in your favor. They will then turn eagerly to your Argument to read the legal support for the result they have already come to believe is just.

Start with your strongest argument whenever possible. If a comedian's first joke is funny, you laugh more easily at those that follow. If a band's first song is good, you listen more generously to those that follow. If your first argument is strong, judges will read those that follow with more attention and respect. If it's weak, they will assume what follows is even weaker. Their interest will flag. They may skim. They may even stop.

Don't squander the momentum you've built with your facts. The facts should have put the court in the mood to buy your arguments. If possible, your first argument should close the deal. Don't go for a slow build. Start with the argument most likely to win the case for you.

If you're writing a responsive memorandum or brief, don't feel bound to follow the order of issues used by your opponent. If it suits your purposes, fine. Your memorandum or brief will be easy to understand if it matches your opponent's. But if following your opponent's order compromises your persuasive strategy, go your own way. Pick an order that reflects your view of the case and highlights your strengths.

Unfortunately, logic or sound strategy may require you to start with other than your strongest argument. You may have to start with a procedural issue—like the statute of limitations or standing—on which your case is weak, before you can logically proceed to your stronger arguments on the merits. You may have to start with a weak argument on liability before you can logically proceed to your stronger argument on damages. In a responsive brief, you may have to start with your weakest argument because you know it is the issue on which the appellant is most likely to get your judgment reversed.

In all these situations, keep your eye on the big picture. Your winning argument on an issue will be wasted if you lose the case. Tailor the order of your arguments to the needs of your particular case. If you're lucky, you'll get to put your strongest argument first.

Argue issues one at a time using CRAC. Like an objective discussion of an issue, an argument of an issue should also have a CRAC structure. But while the basic structure will remain the same, obviously the content will change. All the conclusions will be in your client's favor. The rules of law will be presented and applied to your facts in a way that leads to those conclusions. And the arguments supporting your client's position on an issue will come before your refutation of opposing arguments.

Almost everything said about CRAC in the chapter on office memoranda applies equally to CRAC in an argument. CRAC is a flexible tool for organizing your arguments, not an ironclad mold you must squeeze every argument into. Adapt it to your particular argument. For example, in one common adaptation of CRAC, the first conclusion is placed in a point heading and not repeated at the start of the text that follows:

Example 203

I. THE TERMINATION CLAUSE WAS NOT UNCONSCIONABLE UNDER SECTION 2-302 OF THE UNIFORM COMMERCIAL CODE.

A court may refuse to enforce a contract or any part of it that was unconscionable at the time it was made under section 2-302 of New York's Uniform Commercial Code . . . .

The paragraph in Example 203 starts with the rule, because repeating the conclusion from the point heading might seem redundant.

Refute opposing arguments within the framework of your arguments. You can't ignore opposing arguments in the hope the court will do the same. You must confront them. But you don't have to do it on your opponent's turf. By selecting the time and place for the battle, you minimize the damage of adverse authority or facts and maximize your chances of success.

Usually the best place to confront an opposing argument is within the framework of one of your arguments. Avoid starting a section of your Argument by saying the other side is wrong. Instead, start by saying you're right. After you've finished presenting your position, then briefly and efficiently dispose of whatever remains of the opposing argument. Refuting opposing arguments within your framework allows you to maintain the momentum of your argument and to keep your view of the case consistently before the court.

One specific place to do this is at the end of an "A" in a CRAC, after you've applied the rule to your facts in a way that supports your position. The opposing argument would thus be handled in the same place you handled counterarguments in an objective CRAC. To refute an important opposing argument, you might need a complete CRAC. When you do, try to sandwich the CRAC refuting the opposing argument between CRACs presenting your arguments.

Usually you can refute an opposing argument without even mentioning the other side. Don't say:

Example 204
Sportco argues that this case is controlled by <u>Wyatt v. Bach</u>, 949 F.2d 575 (8th Cir. 1991). However, <u>Wyatt</u> is distinguishable because . . . .

Instead, go after the adverse authority directly:

Example 205
<u>Wyatt v. Bach</u>, 949 F.2d 575 (8th Cir. 1991) is inapplicable because . . . .

Avoid presenting an opposing argument in the topic sentence of one of your paragraphs. Don't give the other side so much airtime on your show.

Arguments can be attacked at three levels. The first level is simple accuracy. Search your opponent's argument for the following: (1) a misrepresentation or omission of an important fact; (2) a misquotation of an authority, or an accurate quotation of an authority that's misleading because it's taken out of context; (3) reliance on a case that's been overruled or a statute that's been revised or repealed. If you find one of these, point it out to the court—but only if it's important. Don't nitpick.

The second level is the content of the argument. Point out errors in reasoning within an opponent's argument or inconsistencies between two or more arguments. Distinguish your opponent's cases. Show that the statute was never meant to apply to a case like yours.

The third level concerns the policy implications of the argument. Even though an opposing argument may be accurate and well reasoned, if a decision in the other side's favor would set a dangerous precedent or have harmful practical consequences in the real world, explain that to the court.

Finally, don't look a gift horse in the mouth. If your opponent concedes a point, take advantage of it. And be sure not to waste time arguing a point your opponent has conceded.

Although often you will need to attack your opponent's argument—especially if you are writing a responsive memorandum or brief—generally it's more helpful to concentrate on selling your argument to the court. Picture a guy who's a car dealer. If he spent all his time telling you what lousy cars his competitor was selling, you'd be suspicious. You'd think: "If your cars are so great, why aren't you talking about *them?*" Sell your case.

Choose a few good arguments. When judges give advice to lawyers on persuasive writing, they unanimously recommend avoiding the "shotgun" approach: using a large number of arguments in the hope that one will hit the mark. Using too many arguments creates the impression that no single argument is very good, and the weak arguments detract from the strong. Rely on no more than two or three arguments on an issue. Pick your best shots.

Prefer a simple argument to a complicated one. Judges—and their clerks—are smart people. But they're busy. The shorter and simpler the route of your argument, the more likely they will be to follow you to the end. Scientists and philosophers evaluate arguments using the principle known as "Ockham's razor": The argument that leads to the same conclusion as another but with fewer and simpler hypotheses wins. Apply Ockham's razor when selecting your arguments. Don't let the judges' eyes glaze over.

Offer the court an easy way to rule in your favor. Judges are like everybody else. They want to avoid difficult decisions. They want to avoid unnecessary conflict and controversy.

Accommodate these natural tendencies. Show them the easiest way to reach the result you want. Offer ways to avoid reaching issues that don't have to be reached. Don't ask an appellate court to depart from precedent if the facts of an earlier case can be distinguished. Don't ask the court to overturn a statute if you can show the statute doesn't apply. Be explicit: "If the court finds that Smith's conduct did not come within the statute, the court will not have to reach the constitutional issue." Offer a shortcut.

Add a policy argument if you've got a good one. You won't score any points with a vague argument that something is consistent or inconsistent with "public policy." You must tell the court exactly how a decision in your favor would be good for the real world or the judicial system:

Example 206
An employer must be able to speak freely when giving a job reference about a former employee without fear of being sued for defamation. Otherwise, businesses will not be able to adequately screen job applicants and will mistakenly hire dishonest or unqualified employees.

Example 207
If children can sue their parents for negligence, courts will be flooded with fraudulent claims by families trying to collect insurance under their homeowners' policies.

Show the court how your case fits into the greater scheme of things.

Policy arguments work best with the highest court in a jurisdiction. Intermediate courts of appeal generally see themselves as error correcting courts. Trial courts are even more limited to applying the law as it is. The highest court in a jurisdiction is most free to base its decisions on policy arguments and to change the law when it believes it necessary.

Policy arguments also usually work best in conjunction with arguments based on precedent. But sometimes policy is all you've got. There's an old saying that goes "If you're weak on the law, pound the facts. If you're weak on the facts, pound the law. If you're weak on both, pound the table." If you're weak on the facts and the law, argue policy.

Gear your arguments to the standard of review. To first-year law students, the standard of review often seems like an obscure, abstract, legal technicality. But it is often foremost in the minds of appellate judges, and it can mean life or death to an appeal. The standard of review determines how hard it will be to get an appellate court to reverse the decision of a trial court or administrative agency.

The basic dividing line is between the standard of review applied to issues of law and the standard of review applied to issues of fact. On an issue of law, the appellate court is free to substitute its judgment for a trial judge's judgment. On an issue of fact, the appellate court is much more constrained. It cannot substitute its judgment on a finding of fact unless a trial judge's finding was clearly erroneous, a jury's finding was unreasonable, or an administrative agency's finding was not supported by substantial evidence. Winning an appeal on an issue of fact is therefore much harder than winning on an issue of law.

But this explanation is true only in general terms. There are other standards of review. Complex issues can arise in determining the applicable standard. And the law in this area can change. You must research the particular standard of review applicable to each issue in your case.

Then you must gear your argument on each issue to meet the standard. When the standard favors you—such as when you are the appellee and the appellant is challenging a trial court's finding of fact—it may be your strongest argument. When the standard goes against you, roll up your sleeves.

Rely on a lower court's opinion in your case if it's well-reasoned or well-written. Although a trial court's opinion has no precedential value on legal issues, one in your favor at least shows that a judge agreed with your position. If the lower court was an intermediate appellate court, your reason for relying on its opinion is much stronger. If any lower court's opinion in your case is well-reasoned or well-written, milk it for all it's worth. If the lower court agreed with you on a particular argument, mention that when you make the argument. If the lower court eloquently agreed with you, quote its opinion.

Write in a forceful but reasonable tone. The language you use should convey to the court that you believe in your case. Make strong assertions about your case consistently throughout your argument.

Positive assertions are generally stronger than negative ones. "The contract is consistent with public policy" is stronger than "The contract is not void as against public policy." "The ruling should be affirmed" is stronger than "The ruling should not be reversed."

But you may need to state your assertion negatively when you're tracking the language of a rule or statute. Assume the rule is "A jury's finding cannot be overturned unless it is manifestly contrary to the evidence." If a jury's finding went in your favor, you probably should track the rule, even though it's stated negatively. However, if the jury's finding went against you, you should convert the rule to a positive statement: "The jury's finding can be overturned when it is manifestly contrary to the evidence."

Although you should be assertive, you shouldn't be pushy. Tell the court what it "should" do. Don't tell the court what it "must" do. Don't address the court with naked imperatives like "Reverse the judgment of the trial court" or "Order Sportco to stop violating the contract."

Use restrained language with a tone of reasonableness. Don't label every opposing argument "frivolous," "absurd," or "outrageous." Don't underline every other word. You'll create the impression that you're shouting at the court to distract it from holes in your argument big enough for barge traffic.

Omit needless introductory words at the start of arguments. If you represent Sobel, don't say:

Example 208
It is Sobel's contention that the termination clause was unconscionable under section 2-302.

In Example 208, Sobel's position is a mere "contention," slugging it out on equal footing against the contentions of Greenway. Introductory phrases such as "It is Sobel's contention that" not only add needless words but also weaken the arguments that follow.

You want to create the impression you aren't merely arguing but rather are giving the gospel truth on the particular issue, as mandated by the law and the facts. Sobel's "contention" appears much stronger if you state it without the introductory phrase:

Example 209
The termination clause was unconscionable under section 2-302.

Example 209 looks like a law of physics, fixed and immutable.

Even worse than saying what your client "contends" or "argues" is saying what your client "*could* argue" or "*would* argue." Now your position isn't even an argument, but only an argument you might make. Don't be afraid to make a commitment. *Would* is also weak and unnecessary in such phrases as "it *would* appear" or "it *would* seem." Instead of "*It would appear that* the legislature intended to prohibit such conduct" say "It appears" or "Apparently." If you're reasonably sure, be brave and direct: "The legislature intended to prohibit such conduct."

Finally, don't introduce an argument with "It will be shown that": "*It will be shown that* Rannum had a duty to rescue Massey." When you omit these needless words you make room to say why: "Rannum had a duty to rescue Massey because he was in an area of her property open to the public."

Attack opposing arguments, not opposing lawyers. An opposing lawyer once wrote this about me in a memorandum to a trial court: "If Plaintiff's counsel had read the cases cited in his memorandum, he would have realized they do not stand for the proposition claimed." That made me mad—so mad in fact, that I actually went and read the cases I'd cited. And I doubled my efforts on the case, because my honor was at stake.

If you insult another lawyer, you risk inspiring that lawyer to work harder just to prove you wrong. You also risk alienating the judge, who likes to see lawyers showing respect to one another. So attack the argument, not the lawyer.

Never risk your credibility. If you lose the court's trust, you will lose the case. Honesty is the best policy. Don't hide anything. Give the facts from your client's point of view, but make them accurate and complete. Don't overstate your arguments. Push them only as far as the facts and the law will allow, and not one step further. Acknowledge weaknesses where you must, and show the court how they don't really hurt your case.

Don't risk your credibility with carelessness either. Research thoroughly. Make sure you haven't missed an important case or statute. Make sure you haven't cited a case that's been overruled or a statute that's been revised or repealed. Attend to the details in your writing. A typo, a misspelled or misused word, an incorrect citation, an inaccurate quotation—each may seem trivial, but even a single trivial error can plant the seed of doubt in a judge's mind about your credibility on more substantial matters.

15 Conclusion

Some students complain that the simple and direct style of legal writing doesn't allow them to fully express themselves. But legal writing is not primarily a vehicle for creative self-expression; it is a lawyer's means to specific practical ends. When your client's money, job, health, liberty, or even life is at stake, the most creative writing is the writing that works.

Think of your legal writing teacher as you would a tennis coach. The coach begins by teaching you the basic strokes: the forehand, the backhand, the serve. You wouldn't complain that your tennis coach—by showing you where to position your elbow or where to stand—was inhibiting your freedom of movement on the court. If you want pure freedom of movement, have a few drinks and get on the dance floor. If you want to play tennis and play it well, it takes discipline. So does good legal writing.

But through discipline can come freedom. Once you get good at tennis, the possibilities for self-expression suddenly open up. A well-played match can be a work of art. And the winning shot may be the one you make by throwing your racket at the ball, temporarily abandoning the rules of proper form.

The same thing can happen with your legal writing. Once you master the basics—which this book is designed to teach you—you can go out and do it your way. Abandon the rules when you think something else will work better, but know the rules you are abandoning. Learn to take pleasure in exercising your creativity within a discipline. Write a brief that's a work of art.

16 Selected Readings

Usage and Style

Bernstein, Theodore M. *The Careful Writer.* New York: Atheneum, 1979.

Copperud, R. H. *American Usage and Style: The Consensus.* New York: Van Nostrand Reinhold, 1980.

Follett, Wilson. *Modern American Usage.* New York: Hill & Wang, 1966.

Garner, Bryan A. *A Dictionary of Modern Legal Usage.* New York: Oxford University Press, 1987.

Garner, Bryan A. *The Elements of Legal Style.* New York: Oxford University Press, 1991.

Miller, Casey and Kate Swift. *The Handbook of Nonsexist Writing.* 2d ed. New York: Harper & Row, 1988.

Grammar

Walpole, Jane. *The Writer's Grammar Guide.* New York: Simon & Shuster, 1980.

Citation

The Bluebook: A Uniform System of Citation. 15th ed. Cambridge, Mass.: The Harvard Law Review Association, 1991.

Dworsky, Alan L. *User's Guide to the Bluebook.* 2d ed. Littleton, Colo.: Fred B. Rothman & Co., 1991.

Plain English

Flesch, Rudolph. *How to Write Plain English: A Book for Lawyers and Consumers.* New York: Harper & Row, 1979.

Mellinkoff, David. *Legal Writing: Sense and Nonsense.* St. Paul: West, 1982.

Wydick, Richard C. *Plain English for Lawyers.* Durham, N.C.: Carolina Academic Press, 1979.

Legal Writing and Analysis

Dernbach, John C., and Richard V. Singleton II. *A Practical Guide to Legal Writing and Legal Method.* Littleton, Colo.: Fred B. Rothman & Co., 1981.

Neumann, Jr., Richard K. *Legal Reasoning and Legal Writing.* Boston: Little, Brown & Co., 1990.

Advocacy

Dworsky, Alan L. *The Little Book on Oral Argument.* Littleton, Colo.: Fred B. Rothman & Co., 1991.

Fontham, Michael R. *Written and Oral Advocacy.* New York: John Wiley & Sons, 1985.

Hurd, Hollis T. *Writing for Lawyers.* Pittsburgh: Journal Broadcasting & Communications, 1982.

Peck, Girvan. *Writing Persuasive Briefs.* Boston: Little, Brown & Co., 1984.